into THE fields

Catechist and Teacher Formation for the Whole Community

Styles of Teaching and Learning

Year 2

Spiritual Exercises
by **Dan Schutte**

Diana Dudoit Raiche
General Editor

Tools for Teaching
by **Alison Berger**

Sr. Edith Prendergast
General Editor

Bill Huebsch
General Editor
of ***Into the Fields*** *Series*

TWENTY THIRD 23rd PUBLICATIONS

Twenty-Third Publications

A Division of Bayard

One Montauk Avenue, Suite 200

(860) 437-3012 or (800) 321-0411

www.23rdpublications.com

ISBN-10: 1-58595-591-4

ISBN 978-1-58595-591-6

Library of Congress Catalog Card Number: 2006903012

Printed in the U.S.A.

Contents

General Introduction

Into the Fields: Catechist and Teacher Formation for the Whole Community is rooted in Scripture, liturgy, and the *Catechism of the Catholic Church* and is based on both the *General Directory for Catechesis* and the *National Directory of Catechesis*. Each volume of this three-year program blends spiritual formation with theological content, theory, practice, and suggestions for age-appropriate activities. Each provides you with a comprehensive means of learning and acquiring skills for your teaching ministry. The three volumes are: Year 1, *Basic Catechetical Skills and Attitudes*; Year 2, *Styles of Teaching and Learning*; and Year 3, *Teaching Specific Catholic Topics*.

Each of the ten sessions in each volume begins with a spiritual exercise. These profound experiences combine prayer, meditation, reflection, and a related Scripture-based song. A CD with the music for all ten songs accompanies each book.

Next comes *Theological Content*, an essential ingredient for catechist and teacher formation. The ten sessions in each book introduce the topic and recommend the appropriate booklet(s) from the *Growing Faith Project*, a comprehensive and systematic presentation of the faith based on the *Catechism*.

Tools for Teaching is the formal teaching section, providing the connecting link between spiritual growth, the content of the faith, and the instructional strategies needed to do excellent catechesis.

Following is an outline of the *Into the Fields* "pathway," which shows where each of the above three components fits into the process, plus information about the Large Group Sessions, Ongoing Formation Resources, and available Continuing Education Units.

Step 1. Spiritual Exercises

The *Spiritual Exercises* in *Into the Fields* draw upon the wisdom of St. Ignatius of Loyola. The text was written and the songs composed by Dan Schutte, with Diana Dudoit Raiche as the general editor. The exercises are intended to help you grow in your faith and deepen your relationship with God.

Each exercise is accompanied by a piece of music meant to draw you into the heart of the prayer. The reflections engage your mind and will, stretch your understanding, and draw you nearer to the heart of the Lord. A series of "suggestions for use" help you derive the maximum benefit. Each exercise ends with a "colloquy," a prayer conversation with God. The goal here is to be with the God who loves you far more than you know.

Spend about sixty minutes with the exercise, then ten minutes making notes about your experience. Later, within the large group teaching session, you will be invited to share your personal experiences with others.

Step 2. Theological Content

The *Theological Content* follows the flow of the *Catechism of the Catholic Church* and is complete and comprehensive but in plain English. The author is Bill Huebsch, with Sr. Maureen Shaughnessy, SC, as general editor. Here you will be introduced to the themes covered, and share excerpts from the text.

The purpose here is to study the substance of the Catholic faith in measured, manageable amounts using the *Growing Faith* booklet(s) that apply to the particular session you are covering. Spend at least thirty minutes reading the booklet and doing the exercises and reflections suggested there, making notes as you proceed. Again, while this may be done privately, you may wish to join with others in this process outside the formal teaching session. Later, within the large group teaching session, you will be invited to share insights and questions.

You will benefit most from your study of the *Growing Faith* booklets if you also reflect on the artwork and call outs (words in large script). Ask yourself: what do these words (or this illustration) mean to me?

Step 3. Tools for Teaching

Tools for Teaching offers you practical catechetical skills and concrete strategies that work in real teaching sessions. The author is Alison Berger, with Sr. Edith Prendergast as the general editor.

This section begins with the goal and objectives and a skill to acquire for the session. The text then sets the tone with an optional introductory story or exercise. Part Two helps you reflect on the significance of the topic for catechesis. The three sections of material that follow guide you in implementing the objectives, using theory, practical commentary, and examples, plus strategies for different age levels. Also included are questions for personal use and group discussion to help you integrate what you have learned.

Instructions are provided throughout on how to make the most of the various elements, whether you are studying alone or with a group. Read the appropriate section in *Tools for Teaching* and reflect on the questions before each large group session. This should take about thirty minutes and does not involve any note-taking at this point. The note-taking and sharing will be part of the large group sessions.

Step 4. Large Group Sessions

You will be invited to attend one three-hour-long large group session per topic of *Into the Fields*. This session will follow a specific format through which you will experience and share all three components: *Spiritual Exercises*, *Theological Content*, and *Tools for Teaching*. In this meeting, you will review and share as a group some of the insights and reflections you will be recording in your books. In particular, you will discuss and share the questions in *Tools for Teaching*. These gatherings will help you see *Into the Fields* as a total program that will help you grow both spiritually and professionally. Also at this meeting, your facilitator will initial or sign your book to indicate that you have satisfactorily completed each session.

Step 5. Ongoing Formation

We highly recommend that you use *RTJ: The Magazine for Catechist Formation* as part of your ongoing formation as a teacher or catechist. Each issue will carry special *Into the Fields* articles as well as many other invaluable features and columns, all geared to enhancing your teaching ministry. We also recommend that you visit the official *Into the Fields* website regularly as part of your ongoing formation (www.intothefields.org). There you will find suggestions for resources, specific activities for your faith formation sessions, and valuable links to other related sites.

Step 6. Continuing Education Units

At the beginning of each trimester (ten sessions) of *Into the Fields*, if you are interested in obtaining two CEUs from Loyola University in New Orleans, you can register through your group facilitator. You will obtain the CEUs once the facilitator determines that you have satisfactorily completed all ten sessions. For more information, visit the website: www.lim.loyno.edu/lplc.

Welcome to Year Two

Styles of Teaching and Learning

So, you are starting a new year of teaching! Many fresh experiences await you to help both you and your learners grow as disciples of Christ. Whether you have taught for a few years or several, we hope you will learn from and enjoy the material for this second year of the process *Into the Fields: Catechist and Teacher Formation for the Whole Community*.

Styles of Teaching and Learning forms an essential component of *Into the Fields*. It expands on what you learned in Year 1 and helps you deepen your formation and acquire more skills in leading learners to growth in Christ. The topics covered in Year 2 include walking with Jesus, teaching within the whole community, the discernment of spirits, teaching with stories, guiding learners in prayer, and much more.

Keep this volume close by while you are teaching as well as while you are studying. It's not meant to sit on your shelf!

Remember, for your learners you are a most important figure. You are a living witness of the faith you seek to share with them. Your example speaks volumes. You never know when, through you, the Spirit will touch the hearts of your learners. God's grace works in mysterious ways. Even when a lesson may seem to you to be a complete failure, your kindness, your enthusiasm, and your willingness to speak the truth may make an impression on one or more of those you teach.

So, we hope you will make the most of this information program. It has been prepared with much care, research, and prayer. Then let God's grace do the rest—through you.

Walking with Jesus

We Will Journey in Faith

Prayer is more about learning to listen than it is about having the right words to say. We can listen better when our souls are quiet and receptive. And so we begin each of these spiritual exercises with a brief time of centering.

Close your eyes and focus your attention on your breathing. Take several long and slow deep breaths. Imagine that you are breathing in the goodness of God's Spirit, and breathing out all that troubles you. Spend a few minutes with this.

The music for this exercise, "We Will Journey in Faith" (track 1 on the CD), is a song of anointing. Listen to it once with your eyes closed and let the music and words wash over you like a gentle summer breeze. Spend a few moments of quiet at the end.

Now listen to the song again. This time read the lyrics as they are sung. Pay attention to any words, images, or feelings that the song suggests. Also pay close attention to any feelings or memories you resist as you listen, since these sometimes point to ways that you might be resisting the work of God's Spirit. When you've finish, take a few moments to write these down in the empty space.

Here are the lyrics of the song:

We will journey in faith by the light of Christ
And will live by his gospel in spirit and truth.

Let us speak with our lips the peace of Christ,
The healing and hope of our God.

We behold with our eyes the face of Christ,
Who shows us the mercy of God.

Let us bear in our hearts the love of Christ,
The tender compassion of God.

Song Notes

■ ***When you're ready to continue, prayerfully read the following reflection. There's no need to rush through. If there's anything that captures your attention, don't hesitate to stay with it for awhile. Embrace and savor it.***

Under the Banner of Christ

We began these spiritual exercises by reflecting on our desires, those deep hungers that abide in our soul. It is through this soulful hunger that God leads us into deeper intimacy. But it's important for us to also recognize that our desires can sometimes lead us away from God, seducing us to choose things that lead to pride, independence from God, and can, in the end, separate us from our union with Christ.

In each of the exercises, we ask for a particular grace from God. Here it is to become aware of how our desires influence the choices we make. Our inner hunger can lead us toward or away from God. In his *Spiritual Exercises*, St. Ignatius, a soldier before his conversion, envisions the struggle of competing desires to be a matter of spiritual warfare, a battle that engages each of us. It is the battle between good and evil. By the choices we make, we choose to stand in one camp or the other.

We are at any moment being pulled in one direction by our culture of consumerism and power, and at the same time being drawn by the gentle force of grace toward a freedom that allows us in all things to choose God. The attraction of riches, pride, and prestige is powerful. We feel secure and in charge of our lives through our accomplishments and the material things with which we surround ourselves. The only problem with this is that we begin to think of ourselves as independent from God. We can desire to choose a life that is selfish and egotistical, or live in dependence on God, surrendering our own desires into God's hands.

Who will separate us from the love of Christ?

Romans 8:35

Pause for a moment here to reflect on your manner of living and the choices you've made: How does the culture of consumerism play in your life? Do you need things to feel important? Do certain things—the car you drive, the clothes you wear, the people you know—affirm your goodness? Write some of your thoughts in the space below.

Notes

God's Dream

God has a dream for us, for all humanity. Jesus of Nazareth calls it the kingdom of God. The gospel accounts are filled with parables and lessons in which Jesus describes what the kingdom of God is like. This kingdom of peace, justice, and beauty is being built among us through the power of Jesus Christ.

How could we not choose such a dream? Of course we want peace, justice, and the fullness of joy! But it's not about choosing the dream, it's about the strategy used by Christ to bring the kingdom into being. His strategy is to bring about peace and justice by standing alongside those who are outcasts, marginalized, poor, and powerless.

Jesus doesn't embrace this strategy just because it's the harder thing to do. It's not about that. Rather, it's because the dream of God's kingdom is about love. Love is at the heart of it. In God's kingdom there are no outcasts, no marginalized, no poor, no oppressed. Everyone is welcome at the table, not just the rich and the powerful. None of us would choose poverty over riches, humility over honor. But through Christ, our hearts are transformed to see through his eyes and to understand that when we gather at his table, all are welcome. This is Christ's strategy for building the kingdom of God.

In his *Spiritual Exercises*, Ignatius invites a person to "consider Christ our Lord standing in a lowly place."[1] It is his intent that we see ourselves standing there with Christ among the lowly ones, those whom this world rejects and judges as inferior. Jesus embraces humility because it leads to solidarity with those who are embarrassed about their lives. He embraces poverty because it leads to solidarity with the poor and helpless. He rejects earthly honor because it separates him from those who are looked upon as having no status or dignity. We are invited to stand with Christ in poverty, humility, and meekness because this is his strategy to bring about God's dream.

[1]. The *Spiritual Exercises* of St. Ignatius, **No. 144**, The Newman Press

When we allow ourselves to stand with Jesus we allow our hearts to be broken by the same things that break his heart. We allow the poor, the outcast, the forgotten and helpless to affect us, to remind us of our own poverty and helplessness. We receive from them the gift they have for us and we become one. The kingdom of God becomes a reality for us and for them. We've not just preached the message, but we've allowed ourselves to become the message of God's kingdom.

Blessed are the poor in spirit,
for theirs is the kingdom of heaven.
Blessed are those who mourn,
for they will be comforted.
Blessed are the meek,
for they will inherit the earth.
Blessed are the peacemakers,
for they will be called children of God.
(Matthew 5:3–5, 9)

Everyone is welcome at the Lord's table.

Stop here and take some time to ponder your life. Do you allow yourself to know the poor and outcast? Who are the marginalized in your life? Do you allow your heart to be broken by the sorrows of others? Write down your reflections in the space below.

Notes

The Time of Prayer

Close your eyes and imagine yourself in the presence of Jesus. Let him share with you God's dream for humanity. Listen to him and allow your heart to be filled with a desire to share in this dream. When you're ready, continue with the following prayer or with a prayer in your own words.

In the space below, write a few sentences to remind yourself of the graces of this reflection. During the coming week you might also replay the song "We Will Journey in Faith" several times to recall this time of prayer.

God of great kindness,
Fill my heart with love for your least ones.
I want to share your dream
and stand with Jesus in that lowly place
called the kingdom of God.
I am yet so far from embracing poverty and humility,
but I pray that you may gently teach me.
Thank you for loving me so much
and for showing me the tender compassion of God.

When you are ready, end with the Our Father.

The Growing Faith Project booklets for this session are #17 and #18

17 Mystery of the Church

Content summary of booklet #17

- ***The word "church" designates the assembly of those whom God's word convokes, i.e., gathers together to form the people of God.***
- ***The Church in this world is the sacrament of salvation, the sign and instrument of God's communion with us.***
- ***We become members of the people of God through faith and baptism.***
- ***The Church is the body of Christ, the bride of Christ, and the temple of the Holy Spirit.***

This booklet makes reference to articles 748–810 in the *Catechism of the Catholic Church.*

18 Marks of the Church

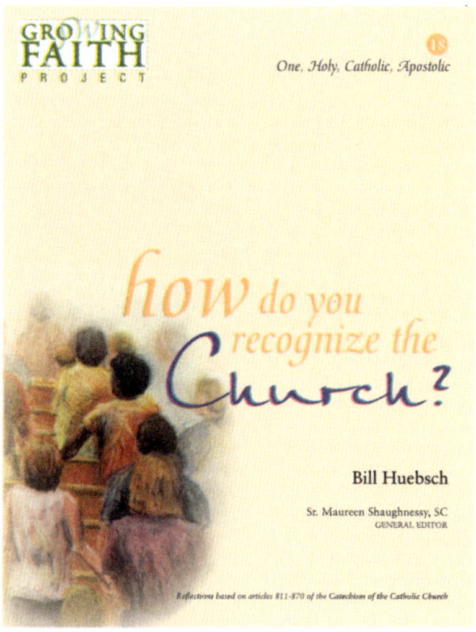

Content summary of booklet #18

- ***The Church acknowledges one Lord, confesses one faith, is born of one baptism, and forms only one body, given life by the one Spirit. Those who do not know Christ or his Church, yet seek God with a sincere heart, may still achieve eternal salvation.***
- ***The Church is holy, founded in Divine Love, the bride of Christ, and filled with grace by the Holy Spirit. While the Church includes sinners, many of her members have attained great holiness.***
- ***The Church proclaims the fullness of the faith to all peoples of all times.***
- ***The Church is built on the foundation of the apostles. Christ governs her through the successors, the pope and the bishops.***

This booklet makes reference to articles 811–870 in the *Catechism of the Catholic Church.*

Excerpt from booklet #17

The people of God

When we say that we are the People of God,
what do we mean?
First, as the name implies,
we are God's People.
And God, we know from Scripture and long tradition,
is love, Divine Love.
This makes us the People of Divine Love.
God who is Divine Love forms us into this people
out of unmistakable and unending love.
Second, one becomes a member of this people
through faith and baptism.

Third, Christ is the head of the Church,
but remember that the Trinity is one God,
Divine Love flowing forth to us,
and that Love Revealed in Christ,
under the anointing of the Spirit of Love.

Christ is the head of the Church.

Teaching within the Whole Community

Goal, Objectives, and Skill

The goal of *Teaching within the Whole Community* is to learn how to involve learners in the life of the community.

Your objectives are

- to gain a strong understanding of the witness of the Christian community as a vital element of catechesis;
- to emphasize the importance of participation in the Sunday Eucharist;
- to learn other methods for involvement in whole community faith formation.

Skill

- Be involved as a learner within the whole community so you will be better able to teach your learners to do the same.

Preparation

- **Step One:** Experience the material in *Spiritual Exercises* and write your reflections.
- **Step Two:** Read booklets #17 *With Whom Do You Gather?* and #18 *How Do You Recognize the Church?* of the *Growing Faith Project*. Complete the reflections and exercises, recording your reflections.
- **Step Three:** Read the *Tools for Teaching* section carefully. It is important to articulate your reflections and applications in writing or verbally, whether alone or working as part of a group. If you are studying with a group, you will also enjoy the opportunity to share your experiences in learning sessions.

Part One: Setting the Tone

This section introduces you to the topic of learning within the whole community. Read and reflect on the sample activity.

Sample Activity: Share a group parable. Have one person begin the parable and continue for one minute. Then ask the next person to repeat what the first person said and continue the story. This pattern will go on until everyone has contributed. The group can help if someone forgets important details of the story.

> The Christian community
> is the origin, *locus*,
> and goal of catechesis.
> GDC 254

Part Two: Importance of This Session

This section outlines and comments on the ways you can involve learners in whole community faith formation. Read this on your own. If you take part in the group sessions, share your reflections with your group.

How do you help learners become part of the faith life of the community?

- Gain a strong understanding of the witness of the Christian community as a vital element of catechesis.
- Emphasize the importance of participation in the Sunday Eucharist.
- Learn other methods for involving learners in whole community faith formation.

Catechesis is the work of the whole community.[1] Catechetical leaders agree that if Catholics, young and old, are to experience real conversion to Christ and lifelong growth in faith, it is necessary to engage in *lifelong learning*. This means that we never really complete our faith formation. In the past, parishes and schools devoted resources exclusively to the faith formation of young people. However, we have come to understand that, in addition to this, we must also invest resources in the faith formation of adults. This is particularly pressing when we consider that all our efforts with young people need to find resonance in their particular households if our comprehensive efforts at faith formation are to bear appropriate fruit.

All our efforts in catechesis seek to bring us more deeply into relationship with Christ, developing our discipleship through the various stages and seasons of our life's journey.

Integrating What You Have Just Learned

- ***What have you done in your religion program to keep persons of all ages involved in faith formation and conversion? Record your reflections and ideas.***

Notes

[1] See GDC 254

tips

- Teach your learners how to really listen. On average most people only listen to (that includes thinking and comprehending), about fifty percent of what is said.
- When possible, arrange for an activity that mingles learners of different age levels. Give the older learners a chance to be mentors for the younger ones.

ON YOUR OWN

- *What do you do to nourish your own faith formation? How do you practice lifelong catechesis in your own life?*

Part Three: Witness of the Community

This section presents the witness of the Christian community as a vital element of catechesis. Read this on your own. If you take part in the group sessions, share your reflections with your group.

The effectiveness of catechesis depends to a great extent on the life of the faith community within which it is carried out. The whole faith community is responsible for making certain that the faith which it seeks to pass on to others, the faith it teaches, preaches, and celebrates, is a faith that is "living, explicit, and fruitful."[2]

When we speak of the witness of the community, we do not speak of a large mass of nameless and faceless people. Our faith community is made up of individuals, some of whom we know, some of whom we don't know. All of us are there to serve one another, to use the gifts God has given us in our journey together, to support each other's faith, and to walk along the road of conversion and commitment to Christ.

This witness and support is important for learners of all ages, for learning and conversion are a lifelong process. These elements are especially important for those who have just been initiated into the Christian community. Newly baptized adults and young people complete their initiation process and expect to join a community with as much energy and love as they have been experiencing in their catechumenate process. Likewise, children taking part in classes or other catechetical gatherings rightly expect their actual community experience to match and express what they have learned. When it does not, the whole enterprise becomes "unbelievable" to them.

> The parish serves as an effective catechetical agent precisely to the extent that it is a clear, living, and authentic sacrament of Christ.
>
> NDC 29C

Hence, the role of the community is vital and essential for catechesis or religious education to succeed.

How do we witness to one another?

- The primary way is by celebrating the liturgy, especially the Sunday Eucharist. The life of the Christian community centers around the Eucharist and the other sacraments. Those who participate in the celebration of the Eucharist share in the Lord's table and worship with their sisters and brothers. A lively, engaging, active liturgy expresses all the beliefs we teach in religious education.
- Another means of witness is the family. The members of a household witness to and share the same faith with one another in their ordinary daily life. What happens at home, after all the study is done, may be the most important element in a child's or young person's formation.
- Honoring the faith of people from other religious traditions expresses the ecumenical spirit of the community. This is especially true when they live within our household.
- Sharing faith, especially by breaking open the Word, is a strong way to build up the faith life of the whole community.
- Finally, serving people in need—whether done as individuals or as part of the parish outreach program—shows learners that faith leads to action.

Integrating What You Have Just Learned

- ***Share with your group or reflect on your own: Who in your community is a model of faith for you? How are you a source of inspiration for others? Write your reflections and ideas.***

Notes

[2] GDC 82

Part Four: At the Lord's Table

Participation in the Sunday Eucharist with the assembly is a powerful witness to the faith. Read this on your own. If you take part in the group sessions, share your reflections with your group.

As already noted, the life of the Christian community centers on the Eucharist and the other sacraments. Every celebration of the sacraments becomes a teachable moment, but the Sunday Eucharist is a powerful moment of whole community catechesis for many reasons.

- In the Penitential Rite we ask forgiveness of God and one another for failing in love.
- Together we hear the word of God and reflect on its meaning for our daily lives. We hear the Word proclaimed and preached, and then we take it with us to live it during the week.
- Our Profession of Faith with the rest of the assembly unites us with one another and with believers who have shared the same faith through the centuries.
- In the General Intercessions we pray for the Church and for the needs of our sisters and brothers around the world.
- At the Offertory, we present bread, wine, and often a financial gift, all symbolic of the "stuff" of our lives, symbolic, indeed, of our very lives. We then offer these gifts to the Father on the altar, praying for the transforming, outpouring of the Holy Spirit so that our lives might be transformed beyond anything we could ever dare to hope for, ask for, or even imagine (see Ephesians 3:20–21).
- The celebration of the Eucharist renews our covenant with God and immerses all of us in the paschal mystery of Christ.
- We offer one another a Sign of Peace to express our desire for reconciliation and unity in Christ.
- Communion is a strong sign of unity. When we receive the body and blood of Christ, we are united with Christ and with one another.

- We are called to realize that we become what we receive and what this implies for our lives. The Eucharist especially commits us to serve the poor.[3]

When our participation in the Eucharist is full, conscious, and active, we enter into the reality of a mystery which is, by its essential nature, profoundly catechetical.

Integrating What You Have Just Learned

- ***Discuss or reflect on your own: Which three of the above points do you think are the most important? Explain. Write your reflections and ideas.***

Notes

[3] See NDC 36A.3

ON YOUR OWN

- *What are the most powerful moments for you in the celebration of the Eucharist and why? After you leave Mass, what moments linger with you longest?*

Part Five:
Involving Learners in the Life of the Faith Community

Other methods of involving learners in the faith community usually require some extra planning and work. Read this on your own. If you take part in the group sessions, share your reflections with your group.

A blind man and a lame man happened to come at the same time to a piece of very bad road. The blind man begged the lame man to guide him through his difficulties. "How can I do that," said the lame man, "as I am scarcely able to drag myself along? But if you were to carry me, I can warn you about anything in the way. My eyes will be your eyes, and your feet will be mine."

"With all my heart," replied the blind man. "Let us serve one another." So he took his lame companion on his back, and the two traveled in this way with safety and pleasure.[4]

Proclamation of the Gospel always begins with the Christian community and invites [learners] to conversion and the following of Christ.
GDC 254

[4] Anthony Castle, *More Quips, Quotes, and Anecdotes*, Twenty-Third Publications

- Serving one another in different ways is an essential element of our Christian life. You might involve learners, according to age level, in some of the social justice or outreach programs being carried on by members or groups in the parish. Some of these could include helping in a soup kitchen, visiting the residents of a nursing home, writing letters to improve laws that affect the poor and homeless, collecting clothes or food, earning money for a particular need, and so on.

- You can give learners an opportunity for a different experience of the faith community through intergenerational gatherings. These gatherings may take different forms, but basically they bring together persons of all ages. The whole group of participants meets for the presentation of a topic. The participants may then form small groups—whether according to age level, by families, or by some other form of division—and discuss the topic. Each small group usually carries out some form of activity related to the topic. The large group may meet together again for a summary/sharing of the small group discussions.

These gatherings can be used for faith sharing on the Sunday readings as well as on the Question of the Week. Learners might also participate in a parish community gathering to celebrate a liturgical season.

- Establishing a prayer hotline can form a connection between learners and members of the faith community.

Strategies for Different Age Levels

You will find ways of bringing learners of different age levels together to celebrate and live their faith. Try these suggestions, and come up with more of your own ideas.

- Invite **primary-age learners** to be prayer partners with persons in the parish. The children might prepare to sing at a community prayer gathering. Teach them about children of other religious beliefs, and have them draw pictures or write "pretend" letters to the children.

- Invite **intermediate-age learners** to take part in a project sponsored by Free the Children, the Holy Childhood Association, or other organizations that help children. They might prepare banners for a parish prayer celebration. Arrange for the children to attend a baptism, and later share about their experience.

- Spend some time with your learners exploring what "ecumenism" means. Lead **middle-school learners, youth, and high-school learners** in planning for an ecumenical event in your parish. This might involve inviting their peers from a local congregation/temple/mosque to attend a liturgy at the parish, and a reciprocal visit by the learners with their families to a liturgy or prayer event at a local congregation/temple/mosque. Each visit might include some time with the priest/minister/rabbi/imam respectively, briefly and appropriately explaining why we pray the way we pray.

- Invite **adults or the participants in intergenerational gatherings** to plan a Parish Cultural Evening or Event. These gatherings might also engage households in celebrating a seasonal tradition such as the blessing of the parish nativity scene, the Way of the Cross, and so on.

As You End This Session

Decide which area of your participation in the faith community is weakest and take a concrete step to improve.

Integrating What You Have Just Learned

- ***Discuss with your group or reflect on your own: What means have you used to involve your learners in the life of the faith community? What has been the result? What are some new approaches or methods you might try? Write down your ideas and reflections.***

Notes

Temptations in the Desert

Give Us Faith, Lord

■ *We begin our time of reflection by centering ourselves in the presence of God. Find a quiet place where you won't be disturbed. Close your eyes for a few moments and breathe slowly as the Spirit of God surrounds you and fills you. Then listen to the song "Give Us Faith, Lord" (track 2 on the CD). Don't work at finding its meaning. Just let it fill you.*

■ *Now listen to the song again. This time follow along as the words are sung and pay special attention to any images or feelings that the song suggests. If any of the words stick out for you, mark them. Our goal is to be authentic before God. If we're bored, irritated, upset, afraid, that's important because that's who we are at this moment. Take a few moments to write your reflections in the space at the right.*

■ ***Here are the lyrics to the song:***

Give us faith, Lord,
when the mountain's too high.
Be our hope, Lord,
when the road is too long.
Teach us love, Lord; Let it blaze
in our hearts and shine to
your glory, O God.

When the shadows of night surround us,
and the darkness has stilled our song,
May the light of your morning bring joy
to our hearts, your grace and love
keep us strong.

When the winters have chilled our spirits,
and we battle our heart's despair,
May the words of your promise rekindle
our hope, renew our trust in your care.

When you bid us to stand before you,
and we tremble before your might,
May we find in your presence the home that
we seek, and live our days in your sight.

When you send us to speak as prophets,
and we waver in doubt and fear,
May the staff of your courage be there at
our side, your song of hope in our ear.

Song Notes

Give me faith
to enter
your world,
your Word.

In this exercise we'll place ourselves with Jesus at the beginning of his public ministry. We know from the gospel stories that Jesus was baptized by John the Baptist in the Jordan River and was then led by God's Spirit into the desert to prepare for his ministry. There Jesus is tempted by the Evil One. We will watch with admiration as he struggles to stay true to his identity as the servant of God who brings the good news that the poor and weak are blessed in God's eyes.

The grace we ask for in this exercise is to know Jesus more intimately as he struggles to follow God's call. We'll again use a kind of prayer that St. Ignatius calls "contemplation." Using the power of our imagination, we enter a Scripture passage, not only to understand it, but beyond that, to actually experience it in our hearts. This kind of prayer takes the story beyond its surface details and allows the story to come alive for us. We become participants.

Read the Scripture account slowly through once.

Then Jesus was led by the Spirit into the wilderness to be tempted by the devil. He fasted for forty days and forty nights, and afterwards he was famished. The tempter came and said to him, "If you are the Son of God, command these stones to become loaves of bread." But he answered, "It is written, 'One does not live by bread alone, but by every word that comes from the mouth of God.'"

Then the devil took him to the holy city and placed him on the pinnacle of the temple, saying to him, "If you are the Son of God, throw yourself down; for it is written, 'He will command his angels concerning you,' and 'On their hands they will bear you up, so that you will not dash your foot against a stone.'" Jesus said to him, "Again it is written, 'Do not put the Lord your God to the test.'"

Again, the devil took him to a very high mountain, and showed him all the kingdoms of the world and their splendor; and he said to him, "All these I will give you, if you fall down and worship me." Jesus said to him, "Away with you, Satan! For it is written, 'Worship the Lord your God, and serve only him.'" Then the devil left him, and suddenly angels came and waited on him. (Matthew 4:1–11)

Where your treasure is,
there your heart will be.
Matthew 6:21

When you feel it's time to draw this part of the exercise to a close, spend a few moments writing down what you experienced. What was most significant for you? What did you feel? What did you learn about Jesus? Did you experience consolation, desolation, or something in between?

Notes

Put the text down, close your eyes, and use your imagination to picture the scene with as much detail as you can. Imagine being in the desert. What does it smell like? What is the air like? Imagine Jesus alone. What is he doing and feeling?

Now begin to hear what's being said and watch as the events unfold. Let the story proceed in whatever way your imagination takes you. The details of the text are not important. If something seems significant, stay with it and don't hurry to move on. Most of all, let your heart feel what's going on. Don't get discouraged if nothing seems to be happening. Sometimes God lets us feel barren and empty to help us realize that it is not in our own power to experience consolation. Try to spend thirty to forty-five minutes with this part.

Feeding the Hunger

Now slowly read through the following reflection.

Jesus' experience of these desert temptations might seem disconnected from our own struggles. After all, have we ever been offered all the kingdoms of the world if we'd only bow down and worship the Evil One? Or been tempted to throw ourselves off a high tower to test God's care?

At their very heart, these temptations are about pride and arrogance. Like the serpent tried with Adam and Eve, the Evil One likes to confuse our thinking about who we really are. We're lured by the dream of thinking that we can be like God, with knowledge of good and evil, controlling the timing and outcome of our lives.

The truth of our lives is that we are not God, but creatures, the work of God's hands. Our very existence is bestowed on us as pure gift. Ultimately we've had nothing to say or do about the miracle of our own birth. We don't control the movement of the stars or the number of days we walk this earth. As was true for Jesus, our glory as creatures lies in our being the beloved of God. Receiving the generosity of his love is our joy. The key is self-acceptance, embracing the glory of who we are but not trying to be something we are not.

We live in pride when we think we've somehow earned the good things in our lives. We live in arrogance when we think we're better than others because of what we've accomplished, how much wealth we've accumulated, or the power we possess. All these things can be taken from us in an instant and are not ours in the first place.

Sometimes the depth of our spiritual hunger can make us desperate. We hate the empty hole in our soul and look for ways to fill it. Unfortunately, the things we choose to fill our hunger are not always good for us. Our contemporary society offers many compelling distractions. For some, accumulating material possessions is an attempt to fill the hunger of the soul. Others will use work, alcohol, medications, sex, or food to deaden the ache in their soul. Rather than depending on God to fill us, we sometimes end up choosing only temporary, hurtful solutions.

Take a moment now to look at how you deal with your own hunger. Ask yourself: Do I treat it with respect and reverence? Do I try to numb the hunger I feel in unhealthy, unholy ways? Write your reflections here.

Notes

The Time of Prayer

■ ***Now take some time to speak to God using the prayer given here, or, better yet, pray in your own words.***

■ ***Take the prayer of this exercise with you in the following days by listening often to the song "Give Us Faith, Lord." Let it remind you of your reflections.***

Kind and generous God,
it is comforting to be with Jesus in his humanity
as he is tempted to forget who he is and what his purpose is.
I am very aware of my pride and arrogance
and how I try to use your gifts to attract attention to myself
or fill the empty place in my soul.
Teach me, dear Lord, to be ever grateful.
Teach me how to receive your gifts with open arms
ever trusting that you will always provide just what I need to
fill my hunger. And subro the thoughts in my head, and seal them to see nothing but good. Fill me with your love, to share with others. Give me hope to fight my trables in Life. Help me help my brothers and sisters that are more in need than me. Give me the gift as well as other to see your compassions as well the Love that you gio us everyday.

When you are ready, end with the Our Father.

The Growing Faith Project booklet for this session is #39

39 The Christian family

Content summary of booklet #39

- ***According to the fourth commandment, God wants us to honor our parents and those to whom he has given authority for our good.***
- ***Children owe their parents or guardians respect, gratitude, just obedience, and assistance.***
- ***Families have the first responsibility for the education of their children in the faith and to provide for the physical and spiritual needs of their children.***
- ***Our duty as citizens is to work with civil authority to build up society in a spirit of truth, justice, solidarity, and freedom.***

This booklet makes reference to articles 2196–2257 in the *Catechism of the Catholic Church.*

Excerpt from booklet #39

The family

In Catholic teaching, marriage has two purposes:
to support the mutual love of the couple
and to bring children into the world.
A man and woman committed in marriage,
together with their children,
form a family.
Other forms of family relationships also exist,
but this is the norm.
Families have many responsibilities and rights
and form the basic building block of society.

This family, together with other relatives,
neighbors, friends, and visitors,
forms a sort of household of faith
and is rightly called a
"domestic church."
We use a particular terminology to refer to families
when we call them a "communion of persons,"
a sign and image of the shared life of the Trinity:
Divine Love,
Love made manifest in Christ,
the Spirit of Love.
Father, Son, and Holy Spirit.
Having children is a reflection of God's work of creation.
Healthy and generous "dying to ourselves" in family life
connects us with Christ in his own dying and rising,
known as the Paschal Mystery.
And being joined in deep unity and solidarity
is a gift of the Spirit to households of faith.
This is a privileged sharing in the life
of the Triune God.

We should honor our parents.

Teaching within the Christian Family

Goal, Objectives, and Skill

The goal of *Teaching within the Christian Family* is to help you learn how to promote the celebration of the faith within the homes of learners.

Your objectives are

- to discover various strategies for involving families in the faith formation experience;
- to encourage means for the growth of the faith within the home, especially by helping families become communities of love;
- to involve family members in the sacramental preparation of the learners.

Skill

- Foster the spiritual growth of the learners' families and households.

Preparation

- **Step One:** Experience the material in *Spiritual Exercises* and write your reflections.
- **Step Two:** Read booklet #39 *What Is a Household of Faith?* of the *Growing Faith Project*. Complete the reflections and exercises, recording your reflections.
- **Step Three:** Read the *Tools for Teaching* section carefully. It is important to articulate your reflections and applications in writing or verbally, whether alone or working as part of a group. If you are studying with a group, take advantage of the opportunity to share your experiences in learning sessions.

Connecting Sessions

In the last session you focused on the whole community as a setting for catechesis. The focus in this session is the Christian family or household as the primary unit of that wider community and as the primary educator of its children.

Part One: Setting the Tone

This optional section introduces you to learning within the Christian family. Read and reflect on this exercise.

In a culture in which time itself is a prized commodity to be carefully hoarded and allocated, consider how we allow the opportunities for family simply being together to be reduced to the level of a commodity. Consider how in the Scriptures there is always a sense that time has a "sacred character" to it, and time spent with others is an affirmation of the holiness of the person. How might we do a better job in our families of honoring each other as "holy," and spending our time together as "sacred time"?

Write down a couple of changes you can discuss with your family or household to give you more time to relax together. Give the reasons for the changes you are suggesting. For example, one family set a day each week for a celebrators evening meal. Another family decided to keep the TV and computer turned off one day or evening a week so they could spend the time conversing. How would you choose to respect family as holy and family time as sacred time?

Parents receive in the sacrament of Matrimony "the grace and the ministry of the Christian education of their children."

GDC 227

Part Two: Importance of This Session

There are some powerful ways that you can promote the celebration of faith within the families or households of your learners. Read this on your own. If you take part in the group sessions, share your reflections with your group.

How do you encourage your learners and the members of their households to respect each other with the gift of sacred time together, time in which they can come to recognize the presence of God in their midst, and perhaps recognize the face of Christ in each other?

- Learn various strategies for involving families in your religion sessions.
- Suggest means for the growth of the faith within the home, especially by helping families become communities of love.
- Involve family members in the sacramental preparation of learners.

As catechists and teachers we certainly appreciate the primary place of the family in the religious formation of learners. When families are actively involved in the parish through participation in the Eucharist, ministry to others, and adult faith formation we know that the learners will be supported in their growth as followers of Christ. However, often families are indifferent, don't find the time, or for other reasons do not take part in the life of the parish. In addition, even families active in the parish community may need help in their celebration of the faith in their own homes. Frequently families are in situations—due to finances, broken relationships, or other causes—that make day-to-day living a challenge.

Our culture is marked by a "degradation of some fundamental values":

- a mistaken concept of the "independence" of spouses;

- a misunderstanding about the relationship of authority between parents and children;
- the growing number of divorces and single parents;
- and the misrepresentation of family life by the mass media.[1]

How can you assist the families of your learners? Some ideas are presented in the following sections.

Integrating What You Have Just Learned

- ***Discuss or reflect on your own.*** *What are some of the difficulties faced by the learners' families or households? What are some of the signs of hope? Write down your ideas and reflections.*

Notes

[1] Cf. Pope John Paul II, *The Role of the Christian Family,* no. 6

ON YOUR OWN

- *What difficulties do you face in your own family or household situation? What are the signs of hope?*

Part Three:
Involving Families in Your Faith Formation Sessions

One way of helping families grow together in discipleship is by involving them in their children's learning activities. Read this on your own. If you take part in the group sessions, share your reflections with your group.

You will discover many ways to let families know what their children or youth are doing in your religion session, but go a step further. In order to help make the household brighter and better, you as a catechist or teacher can actually form a partnership with families or households. Promise to provide their children or youth with the best faith formation. Offer ongoing formation for them through the parish. On their part they promise to take part in what their children or youth are studying. How can you do this?

- If a well-prepared parent's or family's booklet is available with your religion series, make sure each family has a copy.
- Provide "homework" for the households to do with their learners, faith experiences related to the topic the children or youth are studying. For instance, if the topic is prayer, the learners can ask their parents questions such as: what is your favorite prayer? How do you pray? Or ask families to discuss the values depicted on favorite household TV shows. You can give them questions to guide them.
- Invite families to visit one of your sessions to see firsthand what and how the learners are learning.
- Keep in touch with the families to answer questions, provide materials for formation, suggest resources, and so on. You might use your parish email, website, or even a simple newsletter.
- Provide families with faith sharing material (that is, how to share the Sunday readings, how to share about where God is in their lives). In case they don't have a Bible at home, make the readings available on a monthly or weekly basis as well.

Use any or all of these suggestions, or come up with your own, so that you and families can truly minister together to learners.

Integrating What You Have Just Learned

- ***Discuss in your group or reflect on your own: In what ways have you involved parents and families in the learner's faith formation experiences? Which means seems to be the most effective? Record your reflections and ideas.***

Notes

Part Four: Families as Communities of Love

Families can celebrate the faith and help form the faith of their children in the home in various ways. Encourage their efforts and suggest others when possible. Read this on your own. If you take part in the group sessions, share your reflections with your group.

Parents and family members often don't realize that their daily acts of kindness, forgiveness, patience, and care for others are catechetical. All expressions of love teach us something of the nature of the love of God for us.

When a family comes together to make a contribution to the needy, share a family meal, or support one another in a crisis, they are engaging in the practice of love, *caritas*, which is an expression of a well-formed faith. Its habitual practice deepens us in our relationship with God, who first loves us, and it draws us into further relationship with one another.

ON YOUR OWN

- *An excellent resource for faith sharing in households, Exploring the Sunday Readings (Twenty-Third Publications) includes the readings, commentary, and to-the-point family discussion questions.*

When a household celebrates an Advent or Lent tradition or when members of the household express love for one another in different ways, it is another expression of faith shared; it is catechetical. In loving those we see we come to love the One whom we cannot see completely—the God who dwells among us. The household becomes a community of love, building up the Church and transforming the world by God's grace.

Most important is their participation together in the Sunday Eucharist, the communal sacrament of love and unity.

Family or household religious traditions are also a powerful form of catechesis. Every season in the Church's liturgical year carries significant messages. The liturgical year, with all of its richness and wealth of symbols and ritual, reveals the various parts of the one Paschal Mystery of Jesus Christ, and can awaken and nourish the faith of the learners.

The parish can support them in their catechesis by creating a partnership with the family, a covenant in which the parish promises to provide faith formation sessions, a faith-enriching celebration of the Eucharist, and availability to the households. In turn the family or household promises to use the ordinary events of everyday Christian life as catechesis.

Strategies for Families or Households

The various traditions of the liturgical seasons are rituals that involve the whole family or household in a faith experience. Offer these or other suggestions.

Advent: the Advent wreath lighting; the blessing of the Christmas tree; candles in the windows; the Jesse tree; sending Christmas cards; giving gifts to the needy; *las posadas*, the Hispanic celebration of the nine days before Christmas; the Advent calendar.

Christmas: the nativity scene; decorating the Christmas tree; Christmas carols; special Christmas Eve or Christmas Day meals; exchanging gifts.

Epiphany: the celebration of the Three Kings; the blessing of the home; the Three Kings' cake.

Lent: Ash Wednesday; fasting and good works; celebrating reconciliation; following the journey of the catechumens.

The Triduum, the most holy days of the Church year; with special liturgies for each day, culminating in the mysteries of the Easter Vigil and the initiation of the catechumens

Easter: coloring eggs, a sign of new life; mystagogy, entering more deeply into the meaning of the symbols and rituals of the liturgy.

Pentecost: the symbols for the Spirit; celebrating the birthday of the Church.

Mary and the saints: honoring them on their feastdays; praying for their intercession; imitating their example. For **Mary**, especially: the May crowning; the rosary; the Angelus.

Integrating What You Have Just Learned

■ ***With your group or on your own, plan some specific ways you can encourage families or households (including single persons) to "build up communities of love." Choose the three most significant ways for your own family or household at this time and put them into practice. Record your ideas and reflections.***

Notes

ON YOUR OWN

■ *In what ways do you carry on catechesis in your own family or household? Which means seem to be the most effective?*

> Family members learn more of the Christian life by observing each other's strengths or weaknesses than by formal instruction.
>
> NDC 29D

Part Five: Preparing Families for the Journey of Christian Initiation

Sharing in the preparation of their children for the sacraments of initiation—baptism, Eucharist, or confirmation—is a great catechetical moment for families. Read this on your own. If you take part in the group sessions, share your reflections with your group.

When children or youth in your program are preparing to celebrate one or more of the sacraments, their preparation is an excellent teachable moment for families or households. Involving them in one manner or another in the preparation provides faith formation for the adults and bonds the family or household closer together.

Different Strategies for Sacramental Preparation

- **Intergenerational Assemblies** are one approach. The best format for such assemblies is to keep the presentation brief, and prepare interactive experiences that will allow the participants to learn about the symbols of the sacrament, the prayers of the ritual, the ritual itself, and so on. Stations or tables can contain the materials which the family groups visit one at a time in succession. Such an assembly might also include a tour of the parish church. You might also choose to set aside time during which the parents or other adults have their own preparation while the children are involved in a separate activity.

- **Planning a Journey** is another approach. Schedule your meetings around the seasons of the liturgical year. For example, during Advent celebrate First Reconciliation and during the Easter season, celebrate First Eucharist. The meetings could include some with both parents and children, some for parents alone, and some for children alone. For a powerful effect, hold some meetings to which you invite the whole community.

- **Holding a Retreat** is a time-honored way to prepare for the sacraments. The actual make-up of the retreat, the prayers, activities, and so on, may vary, but the experience is prayerful and powerful.

■ **Starting from the Family** is a unique and concrete approach that uses the experience of the family or household as the basis for sacramental preparation. This could include talking about family meals or other household gatherings which are the basis of the eucharistic meal. Family members might discuss the ways they nurture one another, then make the comparison to the larger parish community. They could share how they experience the paschal mystery, for example, through the loss of loved ones, the loss of a job, or the experience of illness, and how these led in some way to the experience of new life. These discussions would be preceded or followed by appropriate activities.

■ **Small Group Work** is an approach that involves parents and one or more catechists, and is especially effective for learners preparing for confirmation. At this age your learners enjoy discussion, outreach activities, and prayer together, and are often able to prepare the prayer celebrations themselves.

As You End This Session

As much as possible, take steps to make your next family or household meal a celebration of unity and joy. Use a seasonal or liturgical theme where possible and appropriate.

Integrating What You Have Just Learned

■ ***In your experience, as a Catholic and a catechist or teacher, which method of preparing for the sacraments is the most effective? How can you incorporate that into your own work? Write your ideas and reflections.***

Notes

The Harvest Is Plenty

Come with Me into the Fields

Begin this exercise by finding a quiet place where you won't be disturbed. Close your eyes and take several slow, deep breaths. Imagine that God's Spirit is entering your body and filling you with peace.

Listen now to the song "Come with Me into the Fields" (track 3 on the CD). Close your eyes and let the music surround you. Don't try to focus too hard or try to figure out the meaning. At the end, allow yourself to be silent for a few moments.

When you're ready, listen to the song again. Follow along as the words are sung and pay special attention to any images or feelings that the song suggests. If anything strikes you as important, make note of it. If you find yourself distracted, it's okay. Sometimes distractions help us know what we should bring to God in prayer. They help us be authentic before God and shouldn't be cause for discouragement. Take a few moments to write down your thoughts in the space provided.

Love bade
me welcome.
George Herbert

Here are the lyrics to the song:

The fields are high and summer's days are few;
Green fields have turned to gold.
The time has come for the harvesting,
For gathering home into barns.

The harvest is plenty; laborers are few.
Come with me into the fields.
Your arms may grow weary;
your shoes will wear thin.
Come with me into the fields.

The seeds they were grown
by other hands than yours;
Nurtured and cared for, they grew.
But those who have sown
will not harvest them;
The reaping will not be their care.

Song Notes

The grace we pray for in this exercise is to know Jesus more intimately. The more time we spend with him, the more we begin to know him. We become attuned to his ways of thinking and to his feelings. The more we know him, the more we are drawn to love him.

We will again use a kind of prayer that St. Ignatius of Loyola calls "contemplation." We will watch Jesus walk along the shore of the Sea of Galilee as he happens upon some fishermen. It's a simple story and one very familiar to us. However, it has profound meaning for us as we get to know Jesus. It's not just a story about some people that lived many centuries ago. We'll use the power of our imagination to experience this story as if it were actually happening to us, as if it's our story.

Begin by slowly reading the Scripture account through once.

> *As Jesus passed along the Sea of Galilee, he saw Simon and his brother Andrew casting a net into the lake—for they were fishermen. And Jesus said to them, "Follow me and I will make you fish for people." And immediately they left their nets and followed him. As he went a little farther, he saw James son of Zebedee and his brother John, who were in their boat mending the nets. Immediately he called them; and they left their father Zebedee in the boat with the hired men, and followed him.* (Mark 1:16–20)

Now put away the text, close your eyes, and imagine yourself on the shore that day. Imagine yourself as one of the fishermen working on the nets. You look up and see this stranger walking toward you on the beach. For some reason you can't take your eyes off him. You expect him to keep on walking but he stops right in front of you. Imagine what he looks like, his face, his eyes. Listen to his voice and what he is saying to you. Let the story unfold in whatever way your imagination takes you. The details of the text are not important. This is your story and it can go however you imagine it. God's Spirit will take your heart just where it needs to go. Don't get discouraged if nothing seems to be happening or if you feel distracted. Sometimes God lets us feel barren and empty to help us realize that it is not in our own power to experience consolation. If this happens during your prayer, simply ask God again for what you desire. Try to spend thirty to forty-five minutes on this part of the exercise.

When you feel it's time to draw this part of the exercise to a close, spend a few moments writing down what you experienced. What was most significant for you? What did you feel? What did you learn about Jesus? Did you experience consolation, desolation, or something in between?

Notes

■ *Now slowly read through and allow yourself to ponder the following reflection.*

Day by Day

Why would they do it? These fishermen, cleaning their boats and mending their nets after a long night, spot a stranger walking toward them on the beach. At first they don't pay much attention. But when he gets close, he greets them and strikes up a conversation. Before they know it, he's asking them to come along with him. And amazingly, they go, leaving behind the only world they've ever known.

How have I let love transform my heart?

Although many details of the story were surely left out of the gospel account, the core of the story is still there. Jesus invited the fishermen to follow him and they went with him. It's hard for us to imagine walking away from our livelihood and following a stranger. What could be so compelling about Jesus to convince them to do such a thing? Perhaps it was something in his voice, in his eyes, that reached into that deep-down hunger in their souls and offered them something they never thought possible.

What is so compelling for you that you choose to follow Jesus? Why are you willing to go where you otherwise might not be willing to go? Take a moment to write your reflections.

Notes

Looking into the Eyes of Jesus

Continue with the reflection, imagining that you are one of the fishermen.

As I listen to Jesus' invitation, I can hear the desire in his voice. "Come, follow me." It's not just that he wants disciples; he needs companionship, my companionship, as he proclaims the good news of God's kingdom. He must know that the path ahead will not be easy, that it will mean loneliness, sleepless nights, and even rejection. He depends on the companionship, the encouragement and comfort of those who are willing to walk with him.

But why would he want me? He has his mission from God. But me, I'm just a fisherman and I don't have eloquent words to speak or teach. I don't have much education. And God knows I've done some pretty bad things for which I'm terribly ashamed. And yet, here he is, looking at me, asking me to be his companion. His eyes seem to look right into my soul.

What is it that keeps me from going with him? Am I afraid to give up the security of my life? Or it could be that I resist walking into an unknown future that takes me to places that are unfamiliar and unsafe. Perhaps I'm just stuck, not willing to take a leap of faith into God's hands. Or maybe I think his message is just some kind of idealistic propaganda that could never solve the problems of the real world.

As those first disciples experienced, following Jesus means our hearts must be transformed, and it is love that changes us. They experienced a profound conversion as the result of meeting Jesus and getting to know him. Little by little, they assimilated the values that they admire in him and tried to emulate the way he lived. When they truly fell in love, it changed them in profound ways.

Take a moment to reflect on what keeps you from saying "yes" to Jesus. Write your reflections here.

Notes

The Time of Prayer

■ ***Now take some time to speak to God using the prayer given here, or, better yet, pray in your own words.***

■ ***Take the prayer of this exercise with you in the following days by listening often to the song "Come with Me into the Fields." Let it remind you of your reflections.***

Good and gentle Lord Jesus,
I listen to your invitation and I am afraid.
I'm afraid of what might happen if I say "yes."
And yet when I look into your eyes,
I see how much you hope that I will come along.
I guess I will need help in responding wholeheartedly.
Please make up for whatever is lacking in my desire.
Teach me how to say "yes."

When you are ready, end with the Our Father.

The Growing Faith Project booklets for this session are #44 and #45

44 Our encounter with God

Content summary of booklet #44

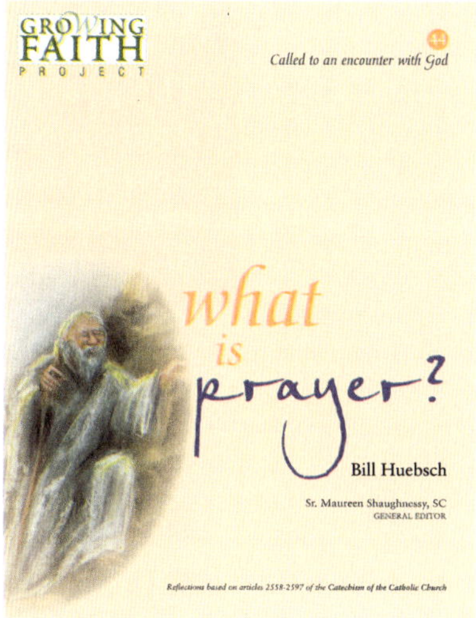

- *In prayer, the Holy Spirit raises our minds and hearts to God.*
- *Prayer is the privileged moment of intimacy with God when we discuss our lives, the needs of the world, and the ways our hearts move within us.*
- *God calls each person to this mysterious encounter.*
- *Prayer unfolds throughout the whole history of salvation as a reciprocal call between God and us.*

This booklet makes reference to articles 2558–2597 in the *Catechism of the Catholic Church.*

45 Forms of prayer

Content summary of booklet #45

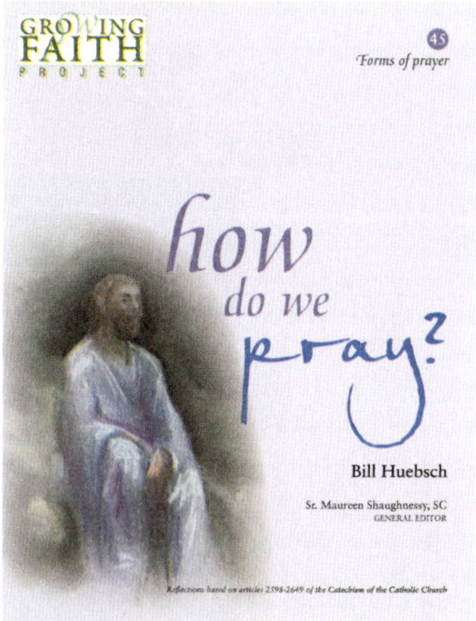

- *The Holy Spirit who teaches the Church and helps us remember all that Jesus said also instructs us in the life of prayer.*
- *The basic forms of prayer are blessing, petition, intercession, thanksgiving, and praise.*
- *The gospels provide an image of Jesus as constantly prayerful.*
- *Because God blesses the human heart, we can in return bless God who is the source of every blessing.*

This booklet makes reference to articles 2598–2649 in the *Catechism of the Catholic Church.*

Excerpt from booklet #44

A surge of the heart

Early in John's gospel is a story that reveals
how Christ stands ready to give us a
drink from the "divine well."
Jesus is speaking with a woman near a well.
He asks her for a drink
and they begin a wonderful conversation.
In it, Jesus teaches her that everyone who drinks
from the well by which they stood
would become thirsty again.

For the water Jesus promised would become a spring,
an inner wellspring,
"gushing up to eternal life!"
This is the wellspring of prayer,
with Jesus as its source
and eternal life as the outcome.

For us Christians,
prayer is the response of faith
to the free promise of salvation
and also a response of love
to the thirst of the only Son of God.

*In prayer,
the Spirit
raises
our minds
and hearts
to God.*

Teaching through Apprenticeship

Goal, Objectives, and Skill

The goal of *Teaching through Apprenticeship* is to help you learn how to find and prepare mentors to assist in the faith formation of learners.

Your objectives are

- to provide suitable mentors for learners;
- to clarify the role of mentors;
- to maintain contact with the mentors.

Skill

- Prepare exemplary mentors to accompany learners.

Preparation

- **Step One:** Experience the material in *Spiritual Exercises* and write your reflections.
- **Step Two:** Read booklets #44 *What Is Prayer?* and #45 *How Do We Pray?* of the *Growing Faith Project*. Complete the reflections and exercises, recording your reflections.
- **Step Three:** Read the *Tools for Teaching* section carefully. It is important to articulate your reflections and applications in writing or verbally, whether alone or working as part of a group. If you are studying with a group, take advantage of the opportunity to share your experiences in learning sessions.

Connecting Sessions

In the last two sessions you learned how to involve learners in the life of the community and how to assist families in the celebration of their faith. Now you will focus on the place of apprenticeship in catechesis.

Part One: Setting the Tone

This optional section introduces the topic of teaching by mentoring.

Read and reflect on your own.

One day when Louis Agassiz was a boy in Switzerland, he and his little brother crossed a frozen lake to join their father. Their mother was watching them and saw in horror a large crack form in the ice. She feared that her younger son would fall in. As she looked on, she saw Louis get down on the ice, his feet on one side of the crack and his hands on the other, forming a bridge. His little brother crept over him to the other side. So may one brother or sister bridge life's dangerous and difficult places for another.[1]

Learning by apprenticeship
is a guided encounter with
the entire Christian life,
a journey toward
conversion to Christ...
a school for discipleship.

NDC 29H

[1] Anthony Castle, *A Treasury of Quips, Quotes, and Anecdotes,* Twenty-Third Publications

Part Two: Importance of This Session

This section develops your objectives for working with mentors for learners. Read this on your own. If you take part in the group sessions, share your reflections with your group.

How do you choose and work with mentors as a catechist or teacher?

- Provide suitable mentors for learners.
- Clarify the role of mentors.
- Maintain contact with the mentors.

Catechesis includes more than instruction. "It must be an integral Christian initiation,"[2] that is, it should include all the aspects of Christian life: knowledge of the faith, liturgical formation, moral formation, and prayer. Dedicated and competent catechists exercise their ministry within certain constraints, however. There is a finite amount of time each week available for catechetical formation. Learners, therefore, need experienced Christian believers to guide them along their journey of discipleship. The RCIA process provides a proven model of such guidance for the youth and adult catechumens preparing for Christian initiation.

Parents or guardians with parental responsibilities are often ideal mentors for their children or youth because of their relationship with them and also because they hold the primary responsibility for sharing the faith with their children. Many adults, however, feel inadequate when it comes to providing a more complete formation for their children. Often, as in the case of parents of different religious beliefs and faith traditions or in the case of single parents overwhelmed with the task of providing for their family, they might not feel that they are in the best position to promote an authentic following of Christ in the Catholic faith.

Parental figures, however, can be coached and affirmed in this role far more than we have perhaps done in the past. But for various reasons it may also be necessary for another suitable mentor to be chosen for the learner. How can you help the mentors, whether parents or others, in their roles? Some ideas are presented in the following sections.

Integrating What You Have Just Learned

- ***Discuss with your group or reflect on your own: who has been a mentor in your own life? When would you imagine your own learners might need mentors? What specifically do you think the role of a mentor would be? Write your reflections and ideas here.***

Notes

[2] Pope John Paul II, *Catechesi Tradendae*, no. 21

tips

- The good example of others has an important place in faith development.

ON YOUR OWN

- *How extensive a role have your godparents (baptismal sponsors) played in your life? Was theirs primarily an "honorary" position?*

Part Three: Who Can Be a Mentor?

The first step in providing mentors for your learners is to discern the role of mentors and, if necessary, which persons are suitable mentors for your learners. Read this on your own. If you take part in the group sessions, share your reflections with your group.

As noted earlier, while the family will remain the primary educator in the faith, parents or caregivers may need coaching and assistance if they are to provide a more complete initiation into the Christian faith, that is, to be mentors for their children.

In other cases the parents will, if possible, assist in choosing a suitable mentor. The mentor could be the child's or youth's godparent (baptismal sponsor), grandparent, aunt or uncle, or a trusted friend from the parish. If the families have no one to recommend, you might suggest someone in the parish who is prepared to carry out this important role.

ON YOUR OWN

- *Which persons have been mentors in your life? How have they helped you?*

What are qualities to look for in a mentor? A mentor would be someone who actively participates in the celebration of Sunday Eucharist, who is a person of prayer and sound judgment, and who relates well to the age level of the learner. A relationship between mentor and learner is characterized by a comfort level and trust that allows for honest communication. A mentor is preferably involved in some form of outreach in the parish. He or she would serve as an example of integrating faith with daily life. A mentor is someone who is comfortable with sharing his or her own faith life and who is willing to engage questions that might be raised by the learner.

It is advisable that both the mentor and the learner make some form of commitment to the process. If a learner is expected to be open to learning from a mentor, a mentor must be open to the possibility of learning from the learner. The learner and the mentor grow *together* in the process that is a journey of faith for both.

Integrating What You Have Just Learned

- ***Discuss or reflect on your own: List some qualities you would look for in a mentor. Be specific but realistic. Write down your reflections and ideas.***

Notes

Part Four: What Does a Mentor Do?

Part four focuses on explaining to mentors their role. Read this on your own. If you take part in the group sessions, share your reflections with your group.

Abraham Lincoln is quoted as saying, "There is just one way to bring up a child in the way he should go and that is to travel that way yourself."

Just what is the role of the mentor? The relationship that usually develops between a catechist and a catechumen provides a perfect model. The mentor is present for each of the learning sessions for families and learners. Mentors usually will meet to talk with the learners and keep in touch with the catechist as the learner progresses.

But the most important part of their role is to guide with both word and example, especially through their own commitment to Christ. The way they talk to the learners, listen to them as persons deserving of respect, answer their questions, help them in a difficult situation, participate in the liturgy, carry out good works, and pray together will impact the learners' lives more than a lecture.

Depending on the schedule and style of your program, the mentors can share in age-appropriate activities with their learners, even some that are not religious in themselves, but which allow the learner and mentor to know one another better and to discuss their faith. Problems can be resolved and growth and awareness will take place.

Strategies for Different Age Levels

Following are some suggestions for activities in which mentors and learners can take part. Some of them may or may not meet your needs, but may inspire other ideas. When the mentor is not a parent, be sure to secure the permission of parents before hosting any activities.

- **For primary-age learners:** Mentors and learners might take a tour of the church together, talking quietly about the various aspects of our faith tradition. They might read and talk about stories together, especially Bible stories, as part of the catechetical experience. If the mentor is also the parent, they can teach the child something the mentor knows how to do, for example, to prepare a meal or set the table.

- **For intermediate-age learners:** Mentors and children might pray together for a special need, writing prayers together as part of the catechetical experience. They might prepare greeting cards for parish members in the hospital. If the mentor is also the parent, they might engage in non-religious activities, sharing time together for fun: fly a kite, take part in a treasure hunt, or let the child teach the mentor something.

- **For middle-school learners, youth, and high-school students:** Mentors and learners might join a Bible study or prayer group together as part of the catechetical experience. They might volunteer to help a needy parish member. When the mentor is also the parent, they can talk about their personal goals and help the learners form a plan of action.

In the end, the role of the mentor is to be an adult or young adult model for the learner. What more powerful way to learn is there?

Integrating What You Have Just Learned

- ***Discuss or reflect on your own:** If you have mentors in your catechetical program, what kind of activities do they share with the learners? Write your reflections and ideas here.*

Notes

ON YOUR OWN

- *Pretend you are a mentor for a child of a certain age. What specific things might you do?*

Part Five: Keeping in Touch with Mentors

You and the mentors should remain in close contact with one another. What are some ways you can do this? Read this on your own. If you take part in the group sessions, share your reflections with your group.

The following poem by an anonymous writer is appropriate for any Christian, but especially for those in the ministry of catechesis.

You are writing a gospel,
A chapter each day,
By the deeds that you do
And the words that you say.

People read what you write,
If it's false or it's true.
Now what is the gospel
According to you?

Maintaining contact with mentors and the families of the learners is essential for integral Christian initiation. The means suggested here are not all-inclusive but may serve as a springboard for your own program.

- **Pray together.** Shared prayer, especially faith sharing based on the Scriptures, is an excellent way for you, the families, and mentors to bond spiritually and to know one another on a deeper level.
- **Meet at appointed times.** These meetings don't need to be frequent but will have a definite purpose and agenda, and in particular, an opportunity to evaluate the apprenticeship process.
- **Use email or phone calls.** These can be more frequent and informal, and used for questions, advice, scheduling, sharing ideas, and so on.
- **Get together.** Enjoy times of relaxation together such as lunches or brunches, watching a game, or just spending part of an evening together, whether it's with all the mentors and catechists, or mentors and families, or all three groups. Just "being together" also offers opportunities for "getting to know you" and informal sharing.
- **Start a simple monthly newsletter or bulletin insert.** Whether done via email, website, or printed, the newsletter is also a good way to keep the community involved. It can include a calendar of meetings, events, prayer intentions, updates, and other information. If your parish already has a newsletter or a website, see if you may have a space for your information.

■ **Do some volunteer or outreach work together, even on a small scale.** Again you may want to team up with other teachers or catechists and mentors. You all have busy schedules, but making time for acts of service is a good way to witness to learners and build up communication and collaboration among your team.

Use your own creativity and the needs of learners and families to find other ways by which mentors can assist the learners and keep in touch.

Comprehensive formation helps the disciples of Christ transform the old person in order to assume their baptismal responsibilities and profess the faith from the heart.

GDC 67

As You End This Session

During the week reflect on the question, "What is the gospel according to me?"

Integrating What You Have Just Learned

■ *Discuss with your group or reflect on your own: Do you use any of the above means for keeping in contact with other catechists and with your mentors? Are there other means you can add to this list? Are there any on the list you would like to try? Write down your reflections and ideas.*

Notes

tips

- Whenever possible, mentors should also be the parents of your learners.
- When mentors are not parents, they should always respect the parents of their learners.
- For a lesson to be effective, the learner has to own it. Let learners come to their own reasonable conclusions.

We Want to See Jesus

Only This I Want

Find a quiet place where you won't be disturbed. Begin by closing your eyes and focusing on your breathing. Inhale slowly and deeply while imagining that the presence of God is filling you. Then exhale slowly as you release any anxiety and tension.

When you feel relaxed, listen to the song "Only This I Want" (track 4 on the CD) with your eyes closed. There's no need to figure out the meaning. Just allow the music to embrace you. At the end, spend a moment in quiet.

When you're ready, listen to the song again. This time follow along as the words are sung. Perhaps there are certain words that strike you, or some image, or a feeling that fills your soul. Make note of anything like this and take a few moments to write your thoughts in the space provided.

Here are the lyrics to the song:

Only this I want: but to know the Lord,
And to bear his cross,
so to wear the crown he wore.

All but this is loss, worthless refuse to me,
For to gain the Lord is to gain all I need.

I will run the race; I will fight the good fight,
So to win the prize of the kingdom of my Lord.

"Only This I Want" by Dan Schutte. From the collection ***Lord of Light***, ©1981, Daniel L. Schutte. Published by OCP Publications, 5536 NE Hassalo, Portland, OR 97213.

Song Notes

The grace we pray for again in this exercise is to know Jesus more intimately. What we experience in these prayerful reflections on Jesus' life is a courtship process. We are day by day coming to know the Lord. As Jesus walks through the towns and villages of Galilee, he is slowly making a home in our hearts and in our lives.

In this exercise we're going to listen to our teacher Jesus, and let his words thrill us and comfort us. As we hear him speak we come to know more of his soul and the depth of his love for humanity. We'll again use the prayer of contemplation to help us enter into the gospel story. This is not pretending or make-believe, but rather a powerful way to experience the words of Scripture. We'll imagine ourselves sitting with the crowds on the hillside on a magnificent summer day, all of us eager to hear what he might have to say to us today. Every time he teaches us it seems our hearts are filled with a deep and abiding joy. Never have we heard anyone else speak like this. By using the power of our imagination we'll experience this story as if it's happening to us right here and now.

In what ways am I blessed?

Begin by slowly reading the Scripture account through once.

When Jesus saw the crowds, he went up the mountain; and after he sat down, his disciples came to him. Then he began to speak, and taught them, saying:
"Blessed are the poor in spirit,
for theirs is the kingdom of heaven.
Blessed are those who mourn,
for they will be comforted.
Blessed are the meek,
for they will inherit the earth.
Blessed are those who hunger and thirst for righteousness,
for they will be filled.
Blessed are the merciful,
for they will receive mercy.
Blessed are the pure in heart,
for they will see God.
Blessed are the peacemakers,
for they will be called children of God.
Blessed are those who are persecuted for righteousness' sake,
for theirs is the kingdom of heaven.
Blessed are you when people revile you and persecute you and utter all kinds of evil against you falsely on my account. Rejoice and be glad, for your reward is great in heaven, for in the same way they persecuted the prophets who were before you."
(Matthew 5:1–12)

Now we'll move more slowly through the passage a second time. As you begin, imagine yourself sitting with the crowd on the side of the hill. What do you see, smell, hear, and feel? Picture people's faces as Jesus begins to speak. The more detail you can imagine the better. Now take the Scripture line by line and allow yourself to experience the wonder of what Jesus is saying. Only move to the next line when you feel you've fully savored the one before. Try to spend thirty to forty-five minutes on this part of the exercise.

Draw this part of the exercise to a close and spend a few moments writing down what you experienced. What was most significant for you? What did you learn about Jesus? What were you feeling?

Notes

As a way of deepening the contemplation, slowly read through the following reflection. Take note of anything that strikes you as significant.

Listening with Our Hearts

When we love someone, we care about what they have to say. We're willing to take the time to listen to what's important to them, what gives them joy and inspires them. And we don't just listen to the words. We let the words penetrate our hearts and change us.

We can imagine Jesus looking out at the faces of these people, asking himself, "What do their hearts need to hear?" He can see their ache and longing, their deep down hunger for God, their pain. Many of them are troubled souls that are empty of hope. Some are in mourning over the death of a loved one or a deep disappointment. There are those who have been deeply hurt by those who've judged them to be unfit, unacceptable, and unworthy of love.

And so Jesus begins to speak to their souls and tells them that all this ache and longing makes a person blessed. Many of them probably expected him to preach about what they need to do to become holy. But he surprises them by telling them that they're already holy and blessed in God's eyes. What a message of hope and freedom this is! Holiness is not about how many prayers I say or how generous I am. It's about being loved and embraced in my poverty, meekness, and hunger. It's about being pure of heart and heralds of peace. And it's about one's willingness to bear insult and rejection for the sake of God's kingdom. This is truly good news.

We might find ourselves resisting some of the things we hear in Jesus' teaching. This is a radical new way of thinking and of looking at life. Are we ready to embrace the mind of Jesus, our friend and brother? Like some of the disciples we may be thinking that this man has to get a more realistic grasp of life. How could he really be serious to count anyone fortunate and blessed who is grieving, meek, or persecuted? Maybe we have a hard time imagining *ourselves* as poor, meek, or pure of heart.

What in Jesus' teaching do you resist? What seems out of sync with your view of the world? Take a moment to write down your reflections.

Notes

■ ***Continue now with the reflection.***

Running the Race

That crowd on the side of the hill surely didn't understand all that Jesus' words meant. But they did sense in his voice a hope that filled them with profound happiness. The heart of the Beatitudes is that we are blessed when we depend on God rather than on ourselves, our talents, our natural gifts, or financial resources. Happiness is found in looking at the world in a new way, Christ's way, where we are the empty vessels that God fills with an abundance of joy.

The freedom of Jesus' message is that we don't have to become something other than we are to be holy and blessed. Favor with God is not found only in times of joy, or being a success, or when we have our lives figured out and under control. It is in being true to ourselves that we are blessed by God.

We have this treasure
in clay jars.
2 Corinthians 4:7

Take a moment to reflect on how you can truly be yourself. Write your reflections here.

Notes

The Time of Prayer

■ ***Now take some time to speak to God using the prayer given here, or, better yet, pray in your own words.***

■ ***Take the prayer of this exercise with you in the following days by listening often to the song "Only This I Want." Let it remind you of your reflections.***

Dearest Lord Jesus,
I come to love and admire you more and more each day.
I don't always understand your words
but I feel great comfort and freedom in them.
You remind me that I don't have to earn God's blessing
but that holiness lies in being myself before God.
Help me, Lord, to see myself as you see me.
I often feel that I am not yet ready to be your disciple,
yet you call me to your side.
Help me to respond with all my heart.

When you are ready, end with the Our Father.

The Growing Faith Project booklet for this session is #47

47 Ways to pray

Content summary of booklet #47

- *The Church invites us to regular prayer: daily prayers, the Liturgy of the Hours, Sunday Eucharist, and the feasts of the liturgical year.*
- *The Christian tradition comprises three major expressions of the life of prayer: vocal prayer, meditation, and contemplative prayer.*
- *The principal difficulties in the practice of prayer are distraction and dryness.*
- *We can always pray; prayer is a vital necessity. Prayer and Christian life are inseparable.*

This booklet makes reference to articles 2697–2758 in the *Catechism of the Catholic Church.*

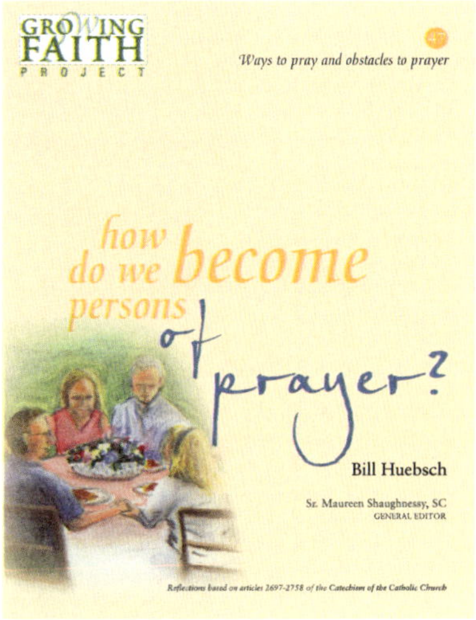

Excerpt from booklet #47

Perseverance in prayer

Love opens our hearts
to three enlightening and life-giving facts
about prayer.
First, it is always possible to pray.
It is possible and even beneficial
to pray at the most ordinary times:
walking alone or with a friend,
seated in a coffee shop,
doing the laundry,
mowing the lawn,
or even while cooking.

Second, prayer is a vital necessity.
Our hearts long for God and are not satisfied
by anything less than communion with the divine.
Third, prayer and the Christian life
are one and the same,
part and parcel of each other.
God is not absent from us and Christ is not distant.
Our prayer is not to a God far away,
but to God who is among us,
radically present,
radically near at hand.

We go to prayer to see what it is that the Spirit
wishes for us.
Pay close attention to the deep mind,
the heart,
the inner voice.
Prayer then makes us attentive to God speaking—
not in many words
or in many unplanned interventions—
but in and through life around us.

Prayer and the Christian life are one and the same....

Teaching with Faith Sharing

Goal, Objectives, and Skill

The goal of *Teaching with Faith Sharing* is to help you learn to use faith sharing as a teaching method.

Your objectives are

- to grasp the dos and don'ts in leading faith sharing;
- to learn how to use examples of faith as a basis for faith sharing;
- to learn how to use questions to engage learners in faith sharing.

Skill

- Engage learners in faith sharing.

Preparation

- **Step One:** Experience the materials in *Spiritual Exercises* and write your reflections.
- **Step Two:** Read booklet #47 *How Do We Become Persons of Prayer?* of the *Growing Faith Project*. Complete the reflections and exercises, recording your reflections.
- **Step Three:** Read the *Tools for Teaching* section carefully. It is important to articulate your reflections and applications in writing or verbally, whether alone or working as part of a group. If you are studying with a group, take advantage of the opportunity to share your experiences in learning sessions.

Connecting Sessions

After studying the relationship between catechesis and the whole community, the family, and apprenticeship, you will now learn specific, practical methods for teaching the faith in your religion sessions. Session 14 teaches you how to use faith sharing.

Part One: Setting the Tone

This optional section introduces the topic of sharing faith. Read and reflect on the story.

An American teacher, a Christian, was employed in Japan on the understanding that during school hours he should not utter a word on the subject of Christianity. The engagement was faithfully kept. He lived among his students as an example of the Christian life but never spoke of it to them. However, so beautiful was his character and so blameless his example, that, unknown to him, forty of his students met and decided to join him in his faith.[1]

Just as God did through that teacher, God prepares the hearts of learners through you to grow in faith and love for Jesus Christ, to lead them to intimacy with him. You are a messenger of God, sent to light other candles.

[1] Anthony Castle, *More Quips, Quotes, and Anecdotes*, Twenty-Third Publications

Catechesis rooted in Sacred Scripture should bring about the discovery of the divine truth it contains and evoke as generous a response as possible.

NDC 67A

Part Two:
Importance of This Session

This section develops your objectives for using faith sharing. Read this on your own. If you take part in the group sessions, share your reflections with your group.

How do you use faith sharing as a teaching method?

- Grasp the dos and don'ts in leading faith sharing.
- Learn how to use stories from our faith tradition or examples from ordinary day-to-day lives as a basis for faith sharing.
- Learn how to use questions to engage learners in faith sharing.

Based on the model of the catechumenate, faith sharing fosters conversion and growth in commitment to Christ. It assists learners in applying the gospel and the truths of our faith to their daily lives. Use faith sharing in some form in each of your religion sessions, whether at the beginning, as part of your prayer experience, or as part of the assimilation of the lesson.

Faith sharing that follows the readings of the liturgical seasons also helps learners be more aware of the themes of the seasons. In reflecting on these themes, the learners are living out the paschal mystery of Christ.

Integrating What You Have Just Learned

- ***Discuss or reflect on your own: With whom do you share your own faith? What value have you experienced in using faith sharing in teaching? Write down your reflections and ideas.***

Notes

ON YOUR OWN

- *How often do you reflect on the meaning of the Sunday gospel for your life?*

Part Three: Leading Faith Sharing

Faith sharing calls for an atmosphere of trust and respect. Read this on your own. If you take part in the group sessions, share your reflections with your group.

How do you form good relationships with your learners? What are some of the qualities you need?

- The ability to listen and to empathize.
- Patience (sometimes lots of it!) and kindness.
- The willingness to put the learners' needs above your own; knowing when to say "no."
- Sharing joys as well as sorrows.
- Recognizing their insights.

(Pause a moment to think of any other qualities.)

- Basically, being a loving, caring person.

If you are going to be a messenger of God, sharing your faith and helping the learners share with one another, you need to show them God's love, and trust and affirm them. No matter what age group you teach, it is important to listen to and learn about them—what they think and feel, how they express themselves. See them as individuals, not just as a group. Teach them to listen to and respect one another's contributions. Then they will feel more comfortable sharing their own faith stories, asking questions, and discussing faith topics.

> The Church imitates
> the Mother of the Lord
> in treasuring the Gospel
> in her heart.
> GDC 78

Keep the following in mind:

- Learners may refrain from sharing for various reasons, for example, family problems, poor self-image, fatigue, and so on. Getting to know the learners' interests, desires, and concerns might help draw them into the conversation. But it's also acceptable for a learner to choose not to share on a particular day.
- Advanced learners are often bored or feel that they already know all the answers. Again, it is important to know the individuals and to challenge them.
- If learners start to share information or stories that seem too personal or confidential, gently suggest that they might share that after your session, if they choose. Always make sure another adult is in the area when you meet with a child.
- If a learner begins crying during a sharing session, pause for a moment of silence and express your empathy in an appropriate way.

Integrating What You Have Just Learned

- ***Discuss with your group members or reflect: What other elements would help build an atmosphere of trust? Write down the results of your reflections.***

Notes

Part Four: Sharing Faith by Presenting Examples

Part four discusses one means of faith sharing. Read this on your own. If you take part in the group sessions, share your reflections with your group.

The first way to share faith, as the story about the American teacher in Japan illustrated, is through example.

- Share with learners (or invite them to share) stories about figures of faith in Scripture, such as Abraham, Sarah, Saint Joseph, and Mary.
- The Church holds up the lives of the saints as examples of living the faith. The saints lived in various historical periods and situations. However, all had in common a great love for God and their sisters and brothers and a heroic practice of the faith.
- There are also contemporary people of faith whose example can inspire learners.

Strategies for Teaching through Examples

You can teach with examples of contemporary figures, saints from our tradition, or biblical characters in various ways, besides sharing their stories.

- Talk about who the saints are and why they are called saints.
- Use different types of activities, according to age level, to help learners apply the examples of the biblical figures and saints to their own lives. For instance, have them role play episodes from the lives of the saints that highlight the virtues of these persons.
- Help them connect the examples of the saints to passages from the gospels.
- Engage older learners in problem solving. Encourage them to reflect: what would St. ________ do if he or she was in this situation (one that learners might face)? How would he or she respond to the needs of the poor and oppressed and to the social injustices of today?
- With younger learners, provide means for interaction when you tell or read the stories.
- Use music related to the message of their lives.
- Show short movies or clips about the saints and discuss them.
- Assign or let the learners choose projects they can create related to the life and/or example of their favorite saints.
- Prepare prayer services or brief prayers centered on a theme from the life of the saint.
- Celebrate the feastdays of the learners' saints, as well as All Saints Day.
- Remember that you and other people in the lives of learners, including the parish community, also teach by your example. Ask learners whom they look up to as models of Christian living and why.

Integrating What You Have Just Learned

- ***Discuss or reflect: What worked and did not work for you in using examples of faith from Scripture or the saints for promoting faith sharing, and why? Write down your reflections.***

Notes

tips

- Establish rules about listening and responding during sharing. Instill respect for one another.

ON YOUR OWN

- *Are the saints real, flesh-and-blood people to you? Explain. How do you relate to them?*

Part Five: Using Questions to Engage in Faith Sharing

The example of Jesus, as well as the process of the catechumenate, offers a model for faith sharing. Read this on your own. If you take part in the group sessions, share your reflections with your group.

Jesus often asked questions, sometimes to make a point, sometimes to engage his listeners in deeper reflection, but always as a call to faith and to conversion. When he spoke about love for enemies, he asked, "For if you love those who love you, what reward do you have? Do not even the tax collectors do the same?" (Matthew 5:46). In talking about setting the right priorities in life, he asked: "Can any of you by worrying add a single hour to your span of life?" (Matthew 6:27). After Lazarus died, Jesus met Martha and told her, "Everyone who lives and believes in me will never die. Do you believe this?" (John 11:26).

In the catechumenate, persons preparing for Christian initiation engage in faith sharing as part of their journey to conversion. They apply the Sunday gospel reading to their own experiences, and each finds personal meaning in the words and actions of Jesus.

Questions leading to discussion are an effective way to begin faith sharing. Base your questions on the Sunday gospel readings, stories, current news events, and so on. Use the parish Question of the Week, which guides the whole community in faith sharing on the Sunday gospel.

Asking questions is an often overlooked skill. We must always intentionally craft our questions in a manner appropriate to the age level toward which our question is directed. All learners need to be guided in discovering the truth for themselves. As they grow older, they will then be able to find in Scripture and Church teaching the answers to the questions with which life presents them. We can begin to help even the youngest children develop this skill.

Strategies for Different Age Groups

Faith sharing requires different approaches for different ages. Try these methods with the learners.

- **Primary-age learners** do not yet have the ability to think abstractly, although they are beginning to form concrete concepts. Third graders may begin to connect concrete concepts to form larger concepts. Questions need to be about specifics in the readings. For example: What did Jesus do? What did he say? What did the prodigal son do? Was that a good thing? What did the father do? Why did the father put his arms around his son and hug him? Was that a good thing? If you were the father (or mother) would you welcome back the son? An activity suited to their age level is often a helpful way to engage them in faith sharing.

- **Intermediate-age learners** are more competent in connecting concrete concepts. Around the age of eleven they begin to develop the ability to think abstractly. Thus the questions you ask or help the learners ask will involve more reflection, for the most part on the concrete level. Again, activities such as simple projects, role-playing, and so on can help them better grasp the message of the reading.

Catechesis should take Sacred Scripture as its inspiration, its fundamental curriculum, and its end because it strengthens faith, nourishes the soul, and nurtures the spiritual life.
NDC 24B

- **Middle-school learners** are able to form conclusions based on abstract thinking. For them, as well as for youth, high school students, and adults, you will want to prepare good, clear, thought-provoking questions according to their age level, questions that will encourage them to share their faith. You can ask open-ended questions and questions that will lead them to make decisions, to move from ideas and beliefs to action. They also will ask questions that can help themselves and their group delve more deeply into the meaning of the Scriptures. Some means for doing this are brainstorming, small group discussions, problem-solving, and simulations in which learners have to make decisions in real-life situations.

- **Adult and young adult learners** can tackle more complex, abstract questions. But it is still best to avoid "theological debate," which can sometimes replace personal sharing. (Invite the learners of all ages to put themselves into the text of Scripture.)

As You End This Session

If you don't already do this, resolve to read and meditate on Scripture at least twice this week, applying its message to your daily life. Better still, do this in a group or with your family.

Integrating What You Have Just Learned

- ***Discuss or reflect on your own: What experiences of faith sharing have you used in your formation sessions?***

- ***How well do you know the developmental level of the learners? In faith sharing, do you also allow room for the action of the Spirit? How? Write your reflections and ideas here.***

Notes

tips

- Keep the sharing moving and active but not undisciplined. One method for doing this is to pass an object, such as a cross, around the circle. Whoever holds the cross takes a turn to either share verbally, or to quietly hold the cross in prayer before passing it on.
- Learn how to keep it within the time limits. Make sure that everyone has a chance to share if they wish.

Lord, Make Me Whole

See the Lilies

Begin this exercise by finding a quiet place where you won't be disturbed. Spend a few moments centering yourself, taking several slow, deep breaths and focusing on the presence of God in you and around you. Release any tension or anxiety as you breathe out.

When you're ready, listen to the song "See the Lilies" (track 5 on the CD), with your eyes closed. Allow the music to enter your soul. Let it comfort and reassure you of God's loving care. At the end, spend a moment in silence to let the song settle inside you.

Now listen to the song a second time. This time follow along with the words as they are sung. If any word, image, or feeling strikes you as significant, make note of it. If you find yourself distracted or even resistant during the song, make note of that, too. Distractions and resistance can often help us to understand things about ourselves that keep us from God. At the end, take a few moments to write down your reflections.

Here are the lyrics to the song:

See the lilies as they grow,
dressed in white like the winter snow.
See their beauty as they sway,
tall and proud in their bright array.
Never was any prince or king
clothed in the splendor of one of these.
Though they never toil or spin
the Lord provides splendid robes for them.

See the sparrows as they fly,
wild and free in the summer sky.
Though they never sow or reap
God provides all the food they need.
Never did any prince or king
dine at the feast given one of these.
God who feeds the sparrow too
will surely care and provide for you.

Seek with joy the reign of God.
Set your hearts on the path of love.
Do not worry what to wear,
what to take as you journey there.
How could the One who clothes the flowers
not understand what your heart desires?
God, who keeps the great and small,
will care for you, most beloved of all.

Song Notes

The grace we ask for in this exercise is to come to know Jesus more intimately, to understand his mind and heart, and to love him more deeply. Today we watch him as he responds with great compassion to a man who cries out for healing. As you read the gospel account use the imaginative prayer of contemplation to enter more deeply into the story. The goal is to allow the scene to become real, as if it were happening right before you. Take the Scripture line by line as you watch the faces and hear what's being said. Let the scene unfold in your imagination. Spend thirty to forty-five minutes with this part.

As he approached Jericho, a blind man was sitting by the roadside begging. When he heard a crowd going by, he asked what was happening. They told him, "Jesus of Nazareth is passing by." Then he shouted, "Jesus, Son of David, have mercy on me!" Those who were in front sternly ordered him to be quiet; but he shouted even more loudly, "Son of David, have mercy on me!" Jesus stood still and ordered the man to be brought to him; and when he came near, he asked him, "What do you want me to do for you?" He said, "Lord, let me see again." Jesus said to him, "Receive your sight; your faith has saved you." Immediately he regained his sight and followed him, glorifying God; and all the people, when they saw it, praised God. (Luke 18:35–43)

Am I willing to let Jesus make me whole?

When you're ready, take a few minutes to write down your reflections. What happened during your prayer? What surprised you? What was most important? What did you come to know about Jesus?

Notes

■ *As a way of deepening the contemplation, now slowly read through the following reflection. Take note of anything that strikes you as significant.*

Lord, I Want to See

It is not easy to admit that we are flawed. We are often embarrassed by our inadequacies, whether it be physical flaw, a mental disorder, or even a spiritual wound. Life is hard and none of us escape some form of brokenness that we wish could be healed. And there are poignant moments when we'd like to cry out to God, "Lord, make me whole again!" We'd like to hope that healing is possible but are told that we should be more realistic and just keep quiet.

The blind man in the gospel story refuses to be silenced by the crowd around him. One can only imagine their tauntings: "Why would he pay any attention to you? Look at your miserable life! Do you really believe that he'd stop to talk with you?" Behind the blind man's persistence is a deep faith that Jesus would listen to his pleas.

But sometimes we just don't want to be healed. We'd rather hold onto the spiritual and emotional hurt we carry for the times we were verbally abused as children, or the abandonment we felt when our spouse walked out on our marriage, or the anger we felt when we were betrayed by a close friend. Some of us grew up in homes of abusive or alcoholic parents whom we struggle all our lives to forgive.

Take a moment to reflect on what in your soul needs healing. Ask yourself: What hurts do I hold inside me? What anger am I unwilling to let go of? What painful memories need the healing of God's love and acceptance? Write down your thoughts.

Notes

■ *Continue now with the reflection.*

The Compassion of God

The first step in healing is realizing how much we are loved. It is so moving to watch how Jesus treats those who are disfigured and broken. Though much of society would like to hide them away in embarrassment, Jesus pays special attention to them and treats them with amazing reverence. He tells the crowd to bring the blind man to him. One can imagine the kindness with which Jesus looks at the man. He doesn't focus on the man's infirmity but simply asks him what he wants. It's such a reverent, loving thing to do.

Jesus never accuses or blames the man for his blindness, even though in that culture this kind of physical infirmity was seen as a punishment from God for some sinful transgression. Healing comes to us when we stop blaming ourselves for the bad things that happen to us.

Our desire is to learn to see with the eyes of Jesus. Take a moment now to reflect on your own way of seeing. How do you treat those who are disfigured, distasteful, or repulsive? Does your discomfort keep you from responding with compassion? How might you become more like Jesus? Write some of your thoughts here.

Notes

Show others the compassion of God.

■ ***When God reaches out to heal, it is not just for the sake of making us whole. God heals us from something so that we might be able to extend healing to the world beyond us. The kindness and compassion of Jesus embraces the blind man so that he in turn may become kind and compassionate toward others.***

In our ministry of teaching we will come across people who are in need of God's compassion and healing. Perhaps what they need most is not so much the knowledge of faith, but rather someone to speak words of encouragement, a friend to hear the hurt they are carrying, or a faith pilgrim who's willing to share their own journey of faith. Great healing can come in sharing our hurts with someone who has also known pain, hurt, and misfortune. Our willingness to pass on the compassion of God is the way we give thanks for the healing that's come to us.

The Time of Prayer

■ ***Close your eyes and imagine yourself in the presence of Jesus. Let him look at you with great love and kindness. When you're ready, continue with the following prayer, or with a prayer in your own words. Speak to God as a friend speaks to a friend.***

■ ***In the space below, write a few sentences to remind yourself of the graces of this time of prayer and reflection. During the coming week you might replay the song "See the Lilies" several times to remind yourself of this time of prayer.***

Dear, gentle Jesus,
I come to you needing to know how much you love me.
Only in your presence can I find the courage to look at my brokenness.
Help me to let the power of your love
reach into those tender places in my heart that need healing.
Let me rest for a moment in the comfort of your embrace.

When you are ready, end with the Our Father.

The Growing Faith Project booklets for this session are #35 and #46

35 Life of grace

Content summary of booklet #35

- *The natural law is our participation in God's wisdom and goodness. It expresses the dignity of the human person and forms the basis of our fundamental rights and duties.*
- *The new law is the grace of the Holy Spirit received in Christ. It is expressed in the words of the gospels and celebrated in the sacraments.*
- *Moved by grace, we turn toward God and away from sin; this journey is called "conversion."*
- *Grace is the help God gives us to become God's own children, intimately bound to the love of the Trinity.*

This booklet makes reference to articles 1949–2029 in the *Catechism of the Catholic Church.*

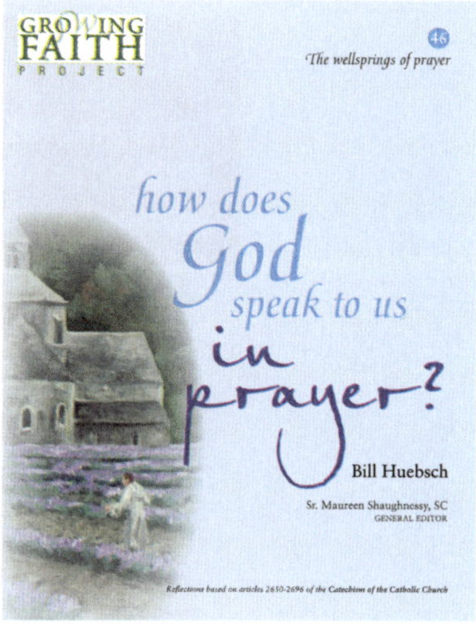

46 Wellsprings of prayer

Content summary of booklet #46

- *The Holy Spirit in the Church teaches us to pray as the children of God.*
- *The word of God, the liturgy of the Church, and the virtues of faith, hope, and charity are sources of prayer.*
- *The different schools of Christian spirituality share in the living tradition of prayer and are precious guides for the spiritual life.*
- *The Christian family is the first place for education in prayer.*

This booklet makes reference to articles 2650–2696 in the *Catechism of the Catholic Church.*

Excerpt from booklet #46

The way of prayer

The way of prayer for the Christian
is always through Christ.
Regardless of the time or place or
method of prayer,
we enter into the divine presence
with Christ as our teacher
and source of grace.

When we pray through Christ,
we use a variety of invocations:
Son of God,
word of God,
Lord and Savior,
Lamb of God,
Good Shepherd,
our Life,
our Light,
our Hope,
or simply, Friend.
But the one name that sums it all up,
the name that is above all others,
the name given at his birth,
is Jesus.
In this name, the divine
and human flow together,
and all faith and love merge.

Mentoring Others in Prayer

Goal, Objectives, and Skill

The goal of *Mentoring Others in Prayer* is to guide learners in prayer, especially by praying with them.

Your objectives are

- to be able to describe what prayer is, using Jesus as your model;
- to make the connection between prayer and the liturgy, the perfect prayer;
- to help learners develop their spirituality through prayer experiences.

Skill

- Help learners develop their spiritual lives, especially through your own example, the example of Jesus, and the liturgy.

Preparation

- **Step One:** Experience the material in *Spiritual Exercises* and write your reflections.
- **Step Two:** Read booklet #35 *Whatever Happened to Grace?* of the *Growing Faith Project* and *#46 How Does God Speak to Us in Prayer?* Complete the reflections and exercises, recording your reflections.
- **Step Three:** Read the *Tools for Teaching* section carefully. It is important to articulate your reflections and applications in writing or verbally, whether alone or working as part of a group. If you are studying with a group, take advantage of the opportunity to share your experiences in learning sessions.

[1] William Bausch, *A World of Stories for Preachers and Teachers*, Twenty-Third Publications

Connecting Sessions

Guiding learners in faith sharing was the goal of your last session. In this session you will focus on a related topic—prayer—as you learn how to help learners develop their spiritual lives.

Part One: Setting the Tone

This optional section introduces the topic of guiding learners in prayer, one aspect of which is knowing how to listen for God's voice. Read and reflect on the anecdote.

At high noon in Manhattan, the streets were, as usual, buzzing with crowds, cars, taxis, horns blowing, brakes screeching, sirens wailing. Two men were making their way together through the crowd. One was a native New Yorker and the other a visiting farmer from Kansas. Suddenly the farmer stopped in his tracks. "Hold on," he said, "I hear a cricket." His friend replied, "Are you kidding? Even if there were a cricket around here, which isn't likely, you would never be able to hear it over all this noise."

The farmer remained quiet for a few moments, then walked over to the corner where a bush was growing in a large cement planter. He turned several leaves over and found the cricket. The city man was flabbergasted. "What good hearing you have!" he exclaimed.

"No," the farmer explained, "it depends on what you have learned to listen for. Look, I'll show you." With that, he pulled a handful of coins from his pocket and let them drop to the sidewalk. As if on signal, every head on the street turned.

"You see," said the farmer, "you hear what you want to hear. It's a matter of what you are listening for."[1]

Part Two: Importance of This Session

This section describes your objectives for helping learners develop their spiritual life. Read this on your own. If you take part in the group sessions, share your reflections with the group.

How can you guide learners in developing their relationship with God?

- Describe what prayer is, using Jesus as your model.
- Make the connection between prayer and the liturgy, the perfect prayer.
- Help learners develop their spirituality through prayer experiences.

Begin by looking at your understanding of prayer and how you can communicate what prayer is in a religious education setting. God calls each of us—religious educators and learners—to a personal relationship. Prayer, then, is our response of faith and love to God's love. It's a way of listening to God, of learning to listen for what God tells us.

The Holy Spirit moves our hearts to prayer and teaches us how to pray. Real prayer comes from the heart, from the center of our being. We withdraw there when we want to meet God, whether in meditation, in a brief prayer moment, or in recognition of God's presence.

The ability to listen is important for our growth in prayer because God can speak to us at different moments through persons, events, nature, difficulties, even painful situations.

How can you share your own experience of prayer with learners in a concrete way? Help learners learn from models of prayer. When you use gestures and symbols drawn from the liturgy, reflect on their meaning. The prayer experiences themselves should also help the learners understand the meaning of the symbols.

Above all, be a person of prayer, for they will learn more from your example than from your words.

Integrating What You Have Just Learned

- ***Discuss with your group or reflect on your own: How has your own prayer life grown over the years? How would you share that experience and understanding with your learners? Write down your reflections.***

Notes

ON YOUR OWN

- *What means do you use to develop your own prayer life?*

Part Three: Jesus, Model of Prayer

Through word and example Jesus teaches us how to pray. Read this on your own. If you take part in the group sessions, share your reflections with your group.

First of all, Jesus' prayer was shaped by his family and his people. " [He learned] to pray from his mother, who kept all the great things the Almighty had done and treasured them in her heart. [He learned] to pray in the words and rhythms of the prayer of his people."[1]

In the heart of his family Jesus learned the ritual of the Passover celebration, which he followed during the Last Supper (Luke 22:7–20). Jesus studied the Scriptures and used them in prayer at home and in the synagogue. The psalms were an important part of the prayer of the Jewish people. Jesus certainly would have known and prayed them daily.

Most important of all, Jesus' prayer sprang from a "secret source": his relationship with his Father. "I thank you, Father, Lord of heaven and earth, because you have hidden these things from the wise and the intelligent and have revealed them to infants" (Matthew 11:25).

When Jesus prayed, he prayed for himself as well as for others: for his apostles, for those who came to him to be healed, for the crowds who gathered to hear his words, for his closest friends. He prayed before the decisive moments of his own mission: at his baptism; during his forty days of fasting in the desert; the night before he chose his apostles; before his transfiguration; at the beginning of his passion. His prayer was in tune with the Father's heart.

Jesus taught us how to pray not only by example but also through parables and stories. Some examples are the parable of the widow and the unjust judge (Luke 18:1–8); the Pharisee and the tax collector (18:9–14); the story of a man who persevered in asking his friend's help (Luke 11:5–13). In his stories, his encounters with people asking for healing and his other teachings, Jesus tells us what he looks for: conversion of heart, love, faith, trust, and watchfulness.

[2] *Catechism of the Catholic Church,* no. 2599

Integrating What You Have Just Learned

■ *Discuss with your group or reflect: How have you used the example of Jesus in talking about prayer with learners? Write down your reflections.*

Notes

Part Four: Prayer in the Liturgy

One source of the Church's prayer is found in the great liturgical traditions of the Church. Read this on your own. If you take part in the group sessions, share your reflections with your group.

Though the formulas of the prayers in the liturgy have changed over the centuries since Jesus' own time, the forms of prayer remain the same: adoration, thanksgiving, contrition, and petition, or, as the *Catechism* words them, blessing and adoration, petition (includes asking forgiveness), intercession, thanksgiving, and praise.

"Blessed are you, Lord God of all creation." This blessing expresses the dialogue between God and us that lies at the heart of prayer. Our blessing is a response to and acceptance of God's gifts. The word "Eucharist" itself means praise and thanksgiving. We give God glory and praise, not for what God does but just because God Is. The Mass is a *living* sacrifice of praise. The Lord Jesus' offering of himself and our personal offering along with his are the center of this celebration.

Two other forms of prayer are petition and intercession. When we petition, we pray for the coming of the kingdom. We pray for all that is necessary to accomplish this, as well as for our own needs: forgiveness, guidance, health, spiritual growth. Intercession is a form of petition. It is prayer for others, as in the General Intercessions or Prayer of the Faithful that is part of every liturgy. Prayers of petition and intercession also form part of the Eucharistic Prayer.

You can help learners see that we can praise, thank, and bless God at any time. The Eucharistic Liturgy, the Mass, is the communal celebration of praise, thanksgiving, and blessing *par excellence*.

Strategies for Different Age Levels

Connect the forms of prayer in the liturgy to life with these activities.

- Help **primary-age children** connect the liturgy and prayer by joining in a litany of blessing, praise, or thanksgiving. Engage them in singing songs of thanksgiving, praise, or intercession. Ask them to draw something for which they are thankful, then have a "thanksgiving parade" around your meeting space.
- Ask **intermediate-age learners** to make a prayer video about persons, events, or situations they would like to pray for, then use it as part of a prayer service. Play a piece or a whole song from a CD with religious instrumental music and ask the children what pictures or reflections came to mind as they listened.
- During your religion session ask **middle-school learners, youth, high-school learners, or adults** to think about some of the things that happened or that they did during the week. Which of these would they offer to God during the Sunday liturgy? Prepare a family meal setting and ask: "As far as prayer goes, how is the Sunday Eucharist like a family meal?" What are the similarities? What are the differences? Why are these worth noticing?

- **In intergenerational gatherings,** ask each family or small group to make a simple banner or mural praising God for different gifts. Place these in the church or in the vestibule. Prepare a Learning Center on the theme: "Prayer in the Liturgy."

Integrating What You Have Just Learned

- *Discuss with your group or reflect on your own: How often and in what ways have you made the connection between prayer and the liturgy in your religion sessions? How can you improve? Write down your ideas and reflections.*

Notes

ON YOUR OWN

- *What does the sentence: "The Mass teaches us how we can give praise to God with our lives" mean to you?*

Part Five: Prayer Experiences

The Church's tradition offers a wealth of prayer experiences you can adopt or adapt for use with learners. Read this on your own. If you take part in the group sessions, share your reflections with your group.

How many different types of prayers and prayer experiences can you find in the Church's tradition of prayer and spirituality?

The Liturgy of the Hours

The Liturgy of the Hours is the great prayer of the Church. The Liturgy of the Hours is prayed throughout the day using psalms and readings from Scripture, so that the "whole course of the day and night is made holy by the praise of God."[3] Each member of the Church is invited to take part according to their situation in life and their calling.

The Liturgy of the Hours centers on the psalms and includes hymns, litanies, and prayers that celebrate the time of day, the liturgical season, and the feast or saint of the day. The reading from the word of God, readings from the Fathers of the Church, the saints and spiritual masters "reveal more deeply the meaning of the mystery being celebrated, assist in understanding the psalms, and prepare for silent prayer."[4]

[3] Second Vatican Council, *Sacred Constitution on the Liturgy*, no. 84

[4] *Catechism of the Catholic Church*, no. 1177

> Prayer is the basis
> and expression of the vital
> and personal relationship
> of a human person
> with the living and true God.
>
> NDC 34

Individual Prayers

- **Prayer formulas** include familiar prayers such as the Lord's Prayer, Hail Mary, the Angelus, and prayers to the saints. They may also include prayers prepared for a particular occasion.
- **Spontaneous prayers** are, as the name suggests, prayers offered "on the spot." They have no preset formula and can be prayers of praise or blessing or petition—any prayer from the heart of the believer.

Scriptural Prayer

- **The reading of Sacred Scripture** should be at the heart of any longer prayer experience.
- **Meditation** is reflection on the word of God (or other spiritual works), applying it to life. Since young learners, including youth, may find it difficult to meditate on their own, **guided meditation** works well with them. In this type of prayer, help the group relax and picture themselves in a pleasant setting. Then, in words suited to the age level, ask them to talk to God, or to Jesus, about the message of the reading. Provide moments of silence so God can speak to their hearts.
- **Journaling** is a means of meditation especially appealing to middle-school learners and youth.
- ***Lectio divina*** is an ancient form of meditation on the word of God, usually experienced on a personal basis but also by groups. It follows a structure of reading, meditation, contemplation, prayer, and action.
- **The psalms** are wonderful prayers that reflect the gamut of human experience and our relationship with God. **Psalm prayers or responses** include verses from the psalms, as well as from the canticles (for example, the Magnificat) and other prayers of the New Testament (for example, the hymn from Paul's Letter to the Philippians, 2:5–11).

Sacramentals

- **Sacramentals** are associated with or imitate the Church's official rituals and celebrate God's presence in daily life. **Devotional prayers** are one category of sacramentals and may be part of personal or group prayer: for example, novenas, litanies, the Rosary, the Way of the Cross, the Sign of the Cross, and others.

- **Rituals** are sacramentals based on the rites or rituals of the liturgy. They engage the group in themes and symbols drawn from the richness of the Church's celebrations, including those that are part of the RCIA process. Two simple examples would be blessing with water and annointing with oil.

Customs and Traditions

- **Song and liturgical movement** (e.g. dance, processions, posture, etc.) are expressions of prayer. These often express something of the customs or traditions of a people. They are especially noteworthy when they raise awareness for us of particular ethnic or cultural groups different from our own. When, at our liturgical celebrations, the diversity of God's people gathers in one voice, one praise, one act of thanksgiving and blessing, we are most richly blessed.

- **Other customs and traditions** that originated in a culture or Church season or both include: the Advent wreath; the blessing of the Christmas tree; the Jesse tree; las posadas; the observance of the feast days of St. Lucy, St. Nicholas, and Our Lady of Guadalupe; the nativity scene; the blessing with ashes on Ash Wednesday; veneration of the cross; the blessed fire; Easter bread; Easter eggs; May altars; and so on.

As You End Your Session

Use a journal to describe moments when you are aware of God's presence in your life.

Integrating What You Have Just Learned

- ***Discuss with your group or reflect on your own: Which forms of prayer have been most effective with the learners you teach and why?***

- ***Are there any mentioned here that you have not tried yet? Are there any you could add to those described above? Write down your reflections and ideas.***

Notes

tips

- Other ways to make prayer time more effective: lighting, music, prayer mats, blessed water, incense, slides, or a sacred image such as a crucifix or icon.
- Pray together at the beginning of the session, at the closing, and even sometimes during the session.

ON YOUR OWN

- *How do you use Scripture in your own prayer?*

Glad Tidings for the Poor

I Found the Treasure

■ *Following the pattern of past exercises, find a quiet place and spend a few moments centering yourself. Close your eyes and take several slow, deep breaths. Imagine that you are breathing the Spirit of God into yourself.*

■ *When you feel prepared, listen to the song "I Found the Treasure" (track 6 on the CD). Keep your eyes closed and simply let yourself experience the music and let the words seep into your soul. Allow for a few moments of silence at the end of the song.*

■ *Then listen to the song again. But this time follow along with the lyrics. Pay special attention to any words, images, or feelings that seem to resonate in your heart.*

■ ***Here are the lyrics for you to follow:***

Lord, to whom can I go?
You alone speak the words of life.
You alone on the earth or in heaven above
are my Savior and my Lord.

I found the treasure in a field,
that neither time nor death can steal.
I will sell what I have, give all that I am,
to hold this treasure as my own.

Jesus, Lord of my life,
I can ask for nothing more
Than to see and believe that my life
lies in you, in the kingdom of my Lord.

■ ***When you've finished, spend a few minutes writing what seemed to be important in your listening.***

Song Notes

■ *Continue by slowly reading through the following reflection.*

Choosing Christ

Our relationship with Jesus Christ is like any of our human relationships. It needs time and attention on our part to keep it healthy and growing. The seed of faith that's been planted in our soul has begun to grow into a flourishing tree, but it needs cultivating, fertilizing, and pruning to help it bear fruit. And so we continue with these exercises to help us do that in a structured way. We give ourselves to this work not only for ourselves but also for those we teach. The word of God is not something that exists on paper; rather, it is a truth that's written in our hearts. It's this living, growing word that we hope to pass on to those entrusted to our care.

How do I cultivate the seed of faith?

It's important that we take the time to examine our lives regularly, to become aware of how we are letting God's word grow in us. In his *Spiritual Exercises*, St. Ignatius encourages us to begin a daily ritual he calls the "examination of conscience." He considered this to be perhaps the single most important spiritual exercise that one can do. Though the "examen" has often been presented as a method of counting our moral shortcomings, Ignatius' purpose is much broader and much more positive than that. In his mind, the purpose of the examen is to become more aware of God's presence in the concrete circumstances of our lives, to look at where he reveals himself during our daily activities. Ignatius understood that the busy pace of our living can be a hindrance to this kind of awareness. And so he encourages us to incorporate this ritual of examining our consciousness into our daily routine.

We speak to God intimately, sharing our thoughts, desires, and actions.

Now take ten to fifteen minutes to do the examination yourself. It's really a very simple process and you can adapt it to your own needs. While seemingly simple, this process can be profoundly helpful for spiritual growth. It's not meant to be a laborious, soul-searching investigation, but a simple act of awareness of God's presence during our day and our response to the urgings of the Spirit. When you're finished, take a moment to write down the results of your examination.

Notes

Here is how the examination works:

- We begin by placing ourselves in the presence of God, who loves us unconditionally.
- We thank God for the good things of our day. These can be simple or profoundly important.
- We reflect on our relationship with God. We look at our thoughts, desires, actions, and omissions to see what they might tell us about our relationship with God and the people in our lives. We pay attention to where we might have resisted God's grace.
- We speak to God intimately, as a friend, sharing our day and asking for the graces of faith, hope, and love.
- We affirm our desire to live our lives gratefully in the presence of God and to open our hearts to his love and grace.

Now continue to read slowly through the reflection.

A Living relationship

It's important to remind ourselves that the most important thing we can pass on to those we teach is a real, living, growing relationship with Jesus. All the rest—the history and doctrine, the understanding of sacraments and grace, the knowledge of Scripture—is quite meaningless if we are not growing in intimacy with Jesus. When we stand up to teach, the most powerful witness we offer is allowing others to see our own growing relationship with Jesus and our sincere desire to grow closer to him.

When he came to Nazareth, where he had been brought up, he went to the synagogue on the Sabbath day, as was his custom. He stood up to read, and the scroll of the prophet Isaiah was given to him. He unrolled the scroll and found the place where it was written:

"The Spirit of the Lord is upon me,
because he has anointed me
to bring good news to the poor.
He has sent me to proclaim
release to the captives
and recovery of sight to the blind,
to let the oppressed go free,
to proclaim the year of the Lord's favor."

And he rolled up the scroll, gave it back to the attendant, and sat down. The eyes of all in the synagogue were fixed on him. Then he began to say to them, "Today this Scripture has been fulfilled in your hearing." All spoke well of him and were amazed at the gracious words that came from his mouth. They said, "Is not this Joseph's son?" (Luke 4:16–22)

Anointed by the Spirit

This passage describes Jesus' mission. As his companions and disciples, it is also our mission. God has anointed us to be the heralds of glad tidings to the poor, to bring sight to the blind, comfort to those in sorrow, and liberty to those imprisoned. But the good news we announce is something that we've already experienced in our own lives, in our own hearts. We understand this because we've been blind, poor, and imprisoned ourselves.

As with Jesus, there may be times when others don't receive what we teach with open hearts. Our students might doubt us, just as people doubted Jesus. Our success or failure as teachers does not depend wholly on our abilities. Sometimes our words fall on fertile soil. Other times they fall on rocky ground. Jesus is the one in charge and has his own time and place for the seed to take root in people's hearts. Our mission is to offer ourselves, with open hearts for ministry, bearing witness to the God we've come to know and love.

The examination can be a powerful way of keeping us aware of our inward journey of intimacy with Jesus. It can also help us reflect on the ways in which our teaching affects our soul. But we need to develop the habit of doing the examination exercise. Take a minute now to make plans about how you might do that. When and where, in the midst of your daily routine, can you do this? What can you do to remind yourself? Write your notes below.

Notes

The Time of Prayer

As in previous exercises, we now end our time of reflection with a colloquy, a heartfelt prayer, in one's own words, in the presence of God. It should be like a friend talking to a friend. Begin with the words provided below, and then continue as your heart may move you. Ask God for what you desire.

If you'd like to make notes to help you recall your time of prayer, you may do that in the space provided. You might want to play the song "I Found the Treasure" often during your week to remind you of this time of reflection and the things you've learned.

Dearest Lord Jesus,
You know my heart and its ways.
You know that my deepest desire is to be close to you,
but sometimes I just don't take the time to pay attention
to you in my life.
When you are alive in my life I know that I am a better teacher.
Help me to be a herald of your good news
to those you entrust to my care.
Help me bring sight to their blindness, hope to their darkness,
and freedom from all those things that imprison their hearts.

When you are ready, end with the Our Father.

The Growing Faith Project booklet for this session is #11

11 Jesus the Messiah

Content summary of booklet #11

- ***The name Jesus means "God saves."***
- ***The title "Christ" means "Anointed One" or "Messiah."***
- ***Jesus Christ is true God and true man, in the unity of his divine person, God incarnate.***
- ***The Incarnation is the mystery of the wonderful union of the divine and human natures in the one person of the Son of God.***

This booklet makes reference to articles 422–483 in the *Catechism of the Catholic Church.*

Excerpt from booklet #11

Who do we say he is?

Anointed by the Spirit in the river,
anointed by God on the mountain,
Jesus Christ is the Messiah.
He was of royal family ties,
born as a descendent of King David.
His teaching and his many works
made clear that he was the
holy one of God.
And he himself came to Nazareth
as a young man,
as Luke's gospel retells it in chapter 4,
to the synagogue, on the Sabbath,
and standing to read,
was handed the scroll
of the prophet Isaiah.

He unrolled the scroll with great purpose
found the passage he wanted,
and read aloud for all to hear.
"The Spirit of the Lord is upon me," he read,
because he has anointed me
to bring good news to the poor...."
His audience was stunned!
And within hours,
or perhaps days at the most,
the work of teaching and healing,
of calling disciples
and shaping them as community,
had begun.

We **proclaim** *that Jesus is* **Lord!**

Teaching with Stories

Goal, Objectives, and Skill

The goal of *Teaching with Stories* is to learn how to use stories effectively in your formation sessions.

Your objectives are

- to value stories as a means of catechesis;
- to become an engaging storyteller, following the example of Jesus;
- to learn different strategies for using stories.

Skill

- Become an effective storyteller.

Preparation

- **Step One:** Experience the material in *Spiritual Exercises* and write your reflections.
- **Step Two:** Read booklet #11 *Who Do People Say that I Am?* of the *Growing Faith Project*. Complete the reflections and exercises, recording your reflections.
- **Step Three:** Read the *Tools for Teaching* section carefully. It is important to articulate your reflections and applications in writing or verbally, whether alone or working as part of a group. If you are studying with a group, take advantage of the opportunity to share your experiences in learning sessions.

Connecting Sessions

In the last session you focused on an important role of the catechist and teacher: how to guide your learners in prayer. This session aims to help you in another role: to become an engaging storyteller.

Part One: Setting the Tone

This optional section introduces the topic of teaching with stories. Read the story once, then reread it, noting the details and how they paint a word picture.

How Rich I Am

They huddled inside the storm door, two children in ragged, out-grown coats. "Any old papers, lady?"

I was busy. I wanted to say no—until I looked down at their feet. Thin little sandals, sopped with sleet. "Come in, and I'll make you a cup of hot cocoa." There was no conversation. Their soggy sandals left marks upon the hearthstone.

After I served them cocoa and toast with jam, I went back to the kitchen to work. The silence in the front room struck me. I looked in. The girl held the empty cup in her hands, looking at it. The boy asked in a flat voice, "Lady, are you rich?"

"Am I rich? Mercy, no!" I looked at my shabby slipcovers. The girl put her cup back in the saucer carefully.

"Your cups match your saucers." Her voice was old and with a hunger that was not of the stomach. They left then. They hadn't said thank you. They didn't need to. They had done more than that.

I moved the chairs back from the fire and tidied the living room. The muddy prints of small sandals were still wet upon my hearth. I let them be. I wanted them there in case I ever forget again how very rich I am.[1]

[1] William J. Bausch, *A World of Stories for Preachers and Teachers*, Twenty-Third Publications

Part Two: Importance of This Session

This section describes tools for building up the faith of learners through stories. Read this on your own. If you take part in the group sessions, share your reflections with your group.

How can you use stories effectively in catechesis?

- Value stories and verbal communication as vibrant means of catechesis.
- Become an engaging storyteller, following the example of Jesus.
- Learn different strategies for using stories.

Stories and storytelling are an ancient form of teaching. Sacred Scripture is full of stories of faith that were handed down for generations. Jesus himself was a great storyteller. He could hold the attention of crowds. He knew how to draw striking word pictures and comparisons, or choose just the right image to communicate a truth.

The parables of Jesus, for example—how much more appealing and memorable they are than a dry explanation. And more, parables are art forms. Like all art forms they have unlimited potential to touch each person individually.[2]

The Church's liturgical year, in particular the readings from the gospels, is an excellent model for storytelling. Each season presents an aspect of the paschal mystery of Christ—his birth, life, miracles, teachings, passion, death, and resurrection. Year after year we never tire of celebrating this life-changing story.

Integrating What You Have Just Learned

- ***Discuss with your group or reflect on your own: What is your favorite parable? What are some of the images it uses? How many lessons does it teach? Write down your reflections and ideas.***

Notes

[2] Sr. Carole Marie Kelly, *A Handful of Fire*, Twenty-Third Publications

ON YOUR OWN

- *Which stories—religious or otherwise—have had an impact on your life? Why?*

Part Three: The Value of Stories

We often use stories without really thinking about their power. Read this on your own. If you take part in the group sessions, share your reflections with your group.

What is the power of stories? Storytelling is the oldest form of communication, yet it is still the best way to teach. Ignatius of Loyola's life was turned around when he read the lives of the saints as he recovered from a serious war wound. An unbeliever, Edith Stein became a Catholic and a Carmelite nun after reading the life and works of St. Teresa of Avila. Stories tell us who we are and where we have come from. They can change our lives.

Good stories remain in our memories like close friends whom we can visit any time. They have many levels of meaning; usually we discover something new every time we read them or hear them told. The greatest movies are also wonderful stories, stories that portray some truth about our lives in an unforgettable way.

The stories of God's love-in-action were handed down from one generation to another by the Chosen People. Jesus' parables and teachings, the stories of his miracles, and, above all, his life, death, and resurrection were first recounted by word of mouth, then later written down by the evangelists. These stories have changed the world and, more than anything else, have impacted its history.

The Church has continued to recognize the value of sharing stories. Through the seasons and feasts of the liturgical year, the Church continues to present the example of Jesus and Mary and of the saints who followed in Christ's footsteps.

Stories can be told in many different ways. In the next two sections you will learn or review some of the methods for telling stories.

Integrating What You Have Just Learned

■ ***Discuss or reflect on your own: What is your experience of engaging your learners with stories? How has this section on the power of stories touched you? Write down your reflections.***

Notes

Part Four: Telling Stories

Learn how to tell stories instead of reading them. Your learners will be delighted. Read this on your own. If you take part in the group sessions, share your reflections with your group.

There are basically three steps in preparing to tell a story.

1. *Preparation*

- Read more than one version of the story; for example, compare a gospel story as it is told by the different gospel writers.

- Look up information about the traditions, geography, family life, foods, even maps of the time and area in which the story takes place. Books filled with information about the life and times of the Bible are available in most libraries.

- Follow in the footsteps of the main character, in this case Jesus; picture the towns, and the hills, hear the waves, see the boats, listen to the birds, smell the flowers and fruit trees, hear the people talking in the shops and on the road.

2. *Simmering*

Let all the information simmer for a while, so you can decide how best to tell the story.

- Usually, telling the story in the first person is the easiest and most effective approach. It allows you to describe the setting and story as someone who actually witnessed them. The more you live with the story, the more you will feel part of it.

- Choose or invent a character you like, someone who fits the story and with whom you feel comfortable. Having a character tell the story also allows you to become someone other than the teacher or catechist. You can express feeling and let the story speak for itself.

3. *Practice*

- Rewrite the story in your own words. Write it as you would tell it; keep it simple with clear images.

- Some persons learn better by hearing, others by seeing. Read the story through several times, putting the pieces of the story together. Did you visualize the story with characters and a setting as though in a movie? Or did you remember the words?

- Try to use both means of learning. Visualize the story in the order it happened. Tape yourself telling the story, so you can test whether you actually do know it. Listening to the tape will also let you hear how you sound, so you can adjust tone, pace, and so on. Then tell the story, the whole story, out loud. Tell it until you own it. The sequence of events is important here. Practice keeping eye contact—this is very important.

You may, of course, choose not to rewrite the story, especially if you are using certain classic children's stories. Even these, if told in a different voice, will give learners a fresh insight into the meaning of the tale.[3]

[3] Diane Crehan, *I Remember Jesus: Stories to Tell and How to Tell Them*, Twenty-Third Publications

Integrating What You Have Just Learned

Discuss with your group or reflect on your own: Have you ever brought a story alive rather than just simply read it? How effective was it? How much preparation did you put into the story? Write down your reflections and ideas.

Notes

tips

- To help prepare for storytelling, use a Bible Concordance to find a word, name, or phrase in the Bible.
- Become familiar with the table of contents of the Bible.

ON YOUR OWN

Have you ever heard a good storyteller recount a story, perhaps a grandparent, someone at a children's library, a homilist? What was the experience like?

Part Five: Having Fun with Stories

Besides actually telling stories, here are some ways you can present all kinds of stories and help learners take part in, review, apply, and assimilate them. Read this on your own. If you take part in the group sessions, share your reflections with your group.

Strategies for Different Age Levels

Primary-age children

- In your focus object corner, place an object related to the story, one that will intrigue the learners.
- Choose stories with concrete imagery. Use some form of pictures, whether pictures from a book or figures on a flannel board or a chalkboard. Create a mural with butcher or shelf paper as a background and use figures and objects torn from paper, cut from fabric, or taken from magazines or calendars.
- Place objects related to the story in a bag and take them out at the appropriate time.
- Use a rebus to tell a story. A rebus is a story combining words with illustrations.
- Involve the children in the story: have them repeat phrases, imitate gestures, or move figures on a flannel board or paper figures on a paper background.
- After you tell the story, involve them in a craft related to the story, have them draw pictures of the story, or you may even want to let them make up a dance or they can act out the story, including dressing up. You can have the children make simple stick or sock puppets to tell the story. They can also retell the story in their own words, referring to the mural or flannel board.
- Another engaging way to review the story is to sing a song related to the story. You can even make up your own song, using a simple children's tune like "London Bridge Is Falling Down."

Intermediate-age children

- Children this age also like to act out stories, but their ability to ad lib and remember the parts of the story is more developed. They also use the story to express their own feelings and understanding.
- They like to look up information about the people in the Bible stories or about the saints or other Christian witnesses. Have the children work on maps, or have them research background information on the people of that time.
- Invite them to make their own more elaborate puppets out of fabric, fake fur, yarn, paper tubes, or flexible foam.
- Have a scavenger hunt for items related to the story, or play a game with words from the story.
- Use pictures related to the story and glue them to cardboard, then cut them into different shapes to form puzzle pieces. Have the children put the pieces together and explain what the connection is between the puzzle and the story.

> Especially in his parables,
> Christ invited his listeners to
> a whole new manner of life.
> NDC 28A.2

Middle-school learners, youth, high-school students, adults

- Small group work is popular with learners of this age level and encourages cooperative learning. Challenge them to look up the stories or parables of Jesus on a certain topic, such as compassion, forgiveness, and so on.
- Pose moral situations appropriate to their age and have them look for an answer in the gospels.
- Invite the learners to role-play their own version of a story. Ask them to come up with symbols for a story.
- Have them share their reflections about the meaning of a story. They can also use journals to record their reflections.
- Challenge your learners to respond concretely to the message of a gospel or other Scripture story with an act of service.
- Assign a photo project based on the message of a story. Encourage learners to be creative and consider the story from different levels.
- Ask learners to make a list of popular songs or TV programs that relate to the message of the story, in either a positive or negative way. They should be prepared to explain their choices.

As You End This Session

Actually prepare to tell a story, following the basic steps given in this session. Tell it in one of your sessions and evaluate the outcome.

Integrating What You Have Just Learned

- *Discuss with your group or reflect on your own: How would you prepare for telling a story? What kind of activity or activities would you use to introduce and help learners assimilate and apply the story? Write down your reflections and ideas.*

Notes

tips

- Telling a story is different from reading one. Put emotion and immediacy into it.
- Look at the faces of your listeners and speak as though from personal experience.

Mercy for All

God of Love

■ *Find a quiet place where you won't be disturbed. Close your eyes and breathe slowly and deeply. Concentrate on your breathing and imagine that you are taking in God's kindness and beauty as you breathe out all that is dark and stressful.*

■ *When you're ready, listen to the song "God of Love" (track 7 on the CD) with your eyes closed. Let the words and music surround you and fill you. Spend a few moments of quiet at the end.*

■ *Now listen to the song again, this time paying special attention to anything that strikes you as important or meaningful. Follow along with the lyrics and note any words, images, or feelings that the song evokes in your soul.*

How do I reveal
the mercy of God?

■ ***Here are the lyrics for you to follow:***

God is love,
and all who dwell in love will live,
Will live in God,
and God will live in them.

All who love are born of God:
our Maker and our Mother.
You have loved us first of all;
yours the love we bear.

We have seen your face, O God,
and we have heard your singing.
We have held you in our hands
in the love we bear.

You have made a home in us
where death can have no power.
We have passed from death to life
in the love we bear.

"God of Love" by Dan Schutte. From the collection ***Lover of Us All***,

■ ***Take a moment to write down what seemed important as you listened to the song.***

Song Notes

Continue by slowly reading through the following reflection.

Embraced by God's Mercy

This is a week where we want to simply rest in the loving embrace of God's unbounded mercy. As we walk through these days we might carry in our hearts the image of God embracing us and offering us unlimited forgiveness. We're again going to use the Ignatian method of contemplative prayer to enter into a gospel story where Jesus extends God's healing mercy to a woman known to be a great sinner. Those present at the table with Jesus are shocked at his response to the woman.

Begin by placing yourself in the presence of a loving God. Then read through the gospel account once to understand the details of the story. Once you've done this, close your eyes and imagine yourself in the house of the Pharisee where Jesus and others have gathered around a table. Imagine what the room looks like. See the people, how they are dressed and where they are seated. In your own way and your own time, let the story unfold before you. The details are not as important as allowing yourself to experience the interaction as if it's really happening to you. Be one of the characters in the story and let yourself feel what's being said and done. The idea is to let the event into your heart so that you are affected by what happens there around that table. Spend thirty to forty-five minutes with this part of the exercise.

> *One of the Pharisees asked Jesus to eat with him, and he went into the Pharisee's house and took his place at the table. And a woman in the city, who was a sinner, having learned that he was eating in the Pharisee's house, brought an alabaster jar of ointment. She stood behind him at his feet, weeping, and began to bathe his feet with her tears and to dry them with her hair. Then she continued kissing his feet and anointing them with the ointment. Now when the Pharisee who had invited him saw it, he said to himself, "If this man were a prophet, he would have known who and what kind of woman this is who is touching him—that she is a sinner." Jesus spoke up and said to him, "Simon, I have something to say to you." "Teacher," he replied, "speak." "Do you see this woman? I entered your house; you gave me no water for my feet, but she has bathed my feet with her tears and dried them with her hair. You gave me no kiss, but from the time I came in, she has not stopped kissing my feet. You did not anoint my head with oil, but she has anointed my feet with ointment. Therefore, I tell you, her sins, which were many, have been forgiven; hence she has shown great love. But the one to whom little is forgiven, loves little." Then he said to her, "Your sins are forgiven." But those who were at the table with him began to say among themselves, "Who is this who even forgives sins?" And he said to the woman, "Your faith has saved you; go in peace."* (Luke 7:36–40, 44–50)

What happened during your time of contemplation? What did you experience? What did you hear or see that you've never noticed before? Was this a time of consolation, desolation, or something in between for you? Take a few minutes to write in the space provided.

Notes

■ ***When you're ready, continue by reading slowly through the following reflection.***

Your Faith Has Saved You

For this woman this was certainly one of life's most embarrassing moments. She must have felt so utterly ashamed and humiliated, and yet is courageous enough to kneel before Jesus. How she was allowed to enter the Pharisee's house in the first place is hard to imagine. And here she is washing Jesus' feet with her tears. What an amazing act of contrition it was! It should remind us of a later time when Jesus himself gets down on his knees to wash the feet of his disciples, an act of unquestionable love and service.

Jesus' reaction to the woman is startling and unexpected by those gathered in the room. He is so tender with her. In an amazingly kind gesture of compassion, he shifts the focus away from the woman and toward the Pharisee who questions his actions. Surprisingly, he doesn't chastise the woman for her sinfulness; but rather, he chastises the Pharisee for his arrogance in judging her actions and judging Jesus himself for receiving her act of contrition. Sometimes we hear the voice of the Pharisee in our hearts because we just can't understand a God who is so generous with his mercy.

Jesus reveals in this story the heart of God. God never spurns us or abandons us. Without hesitation God welcomes us and holds us in the arms of his mercy. It's not important to God that we count our sins or enumerate the details of our sinfulness. The hardest part is for us to overcome our shame and turn to God for forgiveness. We find it hard to believe that God still loves us, even in our sin. We, not God, are the ones who separate ourselves from his love. All we have to do is be ready to receive the unconditional love that's waiting for us.

Holiness is something akin to standing naked and ashamed before God and looking into the eyes of his love. It is that unbounded love, rather than our own efforts, that will transform us from sinner to saint. The glory of our goodness comes from God, not from ourselves. Our joy is indeed great because we are beloved sinners.

The same arrogance we hear in the Pharisee is alive in our hearts when we judge each other. It is not ours to judge, but rather to extend God's forgiveness. Because we've been shown such great mercy, our arrogance is transformed into humble gratitude. In other words, our faith has saved us.

God's love,
not our efforts,
transforms us from
sinners into saints.

Now ask yourself: What area of my sinfulness do I allow myself to separate from God? Of what am I most ashamed? Is there anything that I have a hard time believing that God would forgive? Write your reflections here.

Notes

The Time of Prayer

■ *As in previous exercises, we now end our time of reflection with a colloquy, a heartfelt prayer, in ones own words. This should be like a friend talking to a friend. Begin with the words provided below, and then continue as your heart moves you. Ask God for what you desire.*

■ *Take a moment to make notes to help you recall your time of prayer. You might want to play the song "God of Love" often during your week to remind you of this time of reflection and the things you've learned. As you fall asleep this week, imagine yourself being held in the arms of God's mercy.*

Dearest, most merciful Jesus,
I am overwhelmed with the depth of your love for me.
Sometimes I stay away because it's hard for me to believe
that you would welcome me in my sin.
Forgive my arrogance in not trusting your love.
I'm so grateful, Lord, that you've welcomed me home.
Let me never judge my brothers and sisters
but may I always be ready to embrace them in forgiveness
and extend to them the abundance of your mercy.

When you are ready, end with the Our Father.

The Growing Faith Project booklets for this session are #14 and #

14 The Passion of Christ

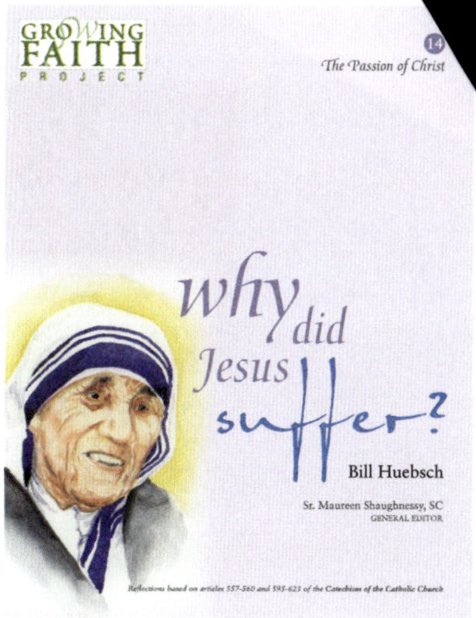

Content summary of booklet #14

- *Jesus' prophetic voice threatened the Church leaders of his day.*
- *The Jews are not responsible for the death of Christ.*
- *Jesus gave us a tremendous sign of his love at the Last Supper when he gave us the gift of himself in the Eucharist.*
- *Jesus freely offered himself for our salvation and died for our sins in accordance with the Scriptures.*

This booklet makes reference to articles 557–570 and 595–623 in the *Catechism of the Catholic Church*.

15 The Risen Christ

Content summary of booklet #15

- *The early followers of Christ experienced him alive among them after his death.*
- *They especially felt his presence while sharing meals. For Christians the sacred meal is Agape, the Eucharist.*
- *In baptism we enter into the death of the Lord, so we can also enter into his resurrection.*
- *Christ now lives with God from whom he came. He opens for us the way to eternal life with God.*

This booklet makes reference to articles 624–682 in the *Catechism of the Catholic Church*.

Excerpt from booklet #15

He is risen!

They began experiencing him again:
in the context of a meal at Emmaus,
or a fish fry on the beach in John's gospel,
or in that upper room among the twelve,
or, as Paul reported, to "more than five hundred
...at one time!"
in 1 Corinthians, chapter 15, verse 6.

Here he is among them,
in his "glorious body"
no longer limited by time and space,
transcending all they could understand.
We are not talking here about a corpse
that has been resuscitated,
as happened to Jairus' daughter,
the son of that widow of Naim,
or Jesus' friend, Lazarus.
Resurrection is not a return to earthly life,
but it is Divine Love
in a new way of being.
Those who experienced him knew Christ now
as filled with the Holy Spirit,
sharing divine life.

g Your Lessons Visual and Active

Goal, Objectives, and Skill

The goal of *Making Your Lessons Visual and Active* is to help you learn when and how to use such aids effectively in your religion sessions.

Your objectives are

- to learn about various symbols and gestures that lead learners into the mystery of Christ;
- to become familiar with the different types of visual aids available for catechesis;
- to learn strategies for making the most of such aids.

Skill

- Choose and use appropriate visual aids to stimulate the attention and imagination of learners.

Preparation

- **Step One:** Experience the material in *Spiritual Exercises* and write your reflections.
- **Step Two:** Read booklets #14 *Why Did Jesus Suffer?* and #15 *Why Do You Look for the Living among the Dead?* of the *Growing Faith Project*. Complete the reflections and exercises, recording your reflections.
- **Step Three:** Read the *Tools for Teaching* section carefully. It is important to articulate your reflections and applications in writing or verbally, whether alone or working as part of a group. If you are studying with a group, take advantage of the opportunity to share your experiences in learning sessions.

Connecting Sessions

Learning how to use stories to teach was the goal of your last session. The skill you are aiming to acquire in this session is closely related to storytelling: how to choose and use appropriate visual media to engage learners in your lesson.

Part One: Setting the Tone

This experience introduces the topic of utilizing visual media to engage the learners. Read and reflect on the following simple exercise.

Read Jesus' teaching about "Do not worry.... Look at the birds of the air....Consider the lilies of the field....Strive first for the kingdom of God" (Matthew 6:25–33). Decide what visuals from this passage you could incorporate in your faith formation sessions.

> Catechetical aids that are faithful to God's Revelation... can be very effective in the hands of skilled catechists.
>
> NDC 71

Part Two:
Importance of This Session

This section describes some of the visuals Jesus used to teach his message. As educators you can follow his example. Read this on your own. If you take part in the group sessions, share your reflections with the group.

How can you use visual media to stimulate the attention and imagination of learners?

- Learn about symbols and gestures that lead learners into the mystery of Christ.
- Become familiar with the different types of visual aids and activities available for catechesis.
- Learn strategies for making the most of them.

Images have been around as long as stories have—in fact, the first stories were told in pictures. Even today, some written languages are based on or are forms of "pictures" (e.g., Chinese, Japanese).

Jesus made good use of concrete images when he taught. He changed the water into wine at the wedding in Cana and so began his public ministry (John 2:11). He used the water in a well to teach the Samaritan woman that he is the living water (John 4:10). He compared the disciples to salt and light (Matthew 5:13–14); he pointed to the birds of the air and the lilies of the field (Matthew 6:26–28). He multiplied the loaves and fish to feed the crowd but also as a sign that he was the bread of life (John 6:35). He used mud to restore the sight of a blind man (John 9:6–7), then spoke of spiritual blindness (John 9:39–41).

Jesus blessed the children and said that "to such as these that the kingdom of heaven belongs" (Matthew 19:13–15). And just as he had allowed John to baptize him in the river (Matthew 3:13–17), he allowed a woman to anoint him in preparation for burial (Matthew 26:12).

In the mystery of his passion, death, and resurrection Jesus gave the ultimate explanation of what he had come to earth for. In his moments of suffering and without words he taught mercy, forgiveness, patience, and, above all, love.

Integrating What You Have Just Learned

- ***Discuss or reflect on your own: What value is there in using visual media? What can you learn from Jesus' example that you can apply to your own situation? Write down your reflections and ideas.***

Notes

tips

- Use visuals that are age appropriate and suited to the needs of your learners as well as to the objectives of your lesson.
- Have all the materials you need well organized and accessible.

ON YOUR OWN

- *What visual media have I made use of? Which ones work best for me and why?*

Part Three: Symbols and Gestures

Catholic liturgy and tradition offer a rich variety of symbols and gestures to help capture the imagination and enhance the understanding of learners. Read this on your own. If you take part in the group sessions, share your reflections with your group.

The Church's liturgy abounds with symbols and gestures that can be used not only for prayer but also to illustrate a gospel passage, a story, or an aspect of the faith. Some of these symbols and their meanings are given below.

- **Bread:** nourishment, Jesus the bread of life, Eucharist, meal, sharing, communion
- **Wine/grapes:** health, sacrifice, blood of Jesus, fruit of the earth, Jesus the vine, communion
- **Water:** new life, cleansing, living water, quenching thirst, baptism
- **Oil:** anointing, healing, appointed to service, strengthening
- **Cross:** faith, Jesus' sacrifice, witness, blessing
- **Candle:** light of faith, Jesus the light, expectation, prayer
- **The altar:** the table of sacrifice, of the eucharistic meal we share, of unity
- **Incense:** prayer, adoration, blessing, purification
- **Bible:** word of God, our faith, God's presence
- **Colors:** purple (penitence, kingly); white (purity, joy, new life); red (the Spirit, blood of Jesus and of the martyrs, witness, love); green (hope, life); gold (celebration, joy)
- **Laying on of hands:** healing, service, invoking the Spirit, blessing

Other symbols represent God

Father: Creator, Pillar of Fire, Cloud, Light

Son: Jesus, Son of God; Savior

Fish: the Eucharist

Shepherd: the one who cares for us

Crown: Jesus the king; *Chi-Rho*: first two letters of Christos; IHS: Jesus, Savior; lamb: the sacrifice and victory of Jesus

Holy Spirit: Wind, breath, dove: sanctifying power, tongues of fire: Pentecost, love, mission (both images taken from Scripture)

Symbols used in catechesis enrich the learners' understanding of the faith and provide multi-layered, visual "insights" into the mystery of Christ and of the Trinity.

Integrating What You Have Just Learned

- ***Discuss or reflect on your own: Suppose you were teaching a lesson on one of the sacraments. How would you use the symbol(s) associated with it as a visual? Write down your reflections and ideas.***

Notes

Part Four: Show and Tell

The visual media and activities available are so numerous that we can only provide a partial listing here. Read this on your own. If you take part in the group sessions, share your reflections with your group.

You have a rich variety of visuals to choose from to spark learners' imagination and interest. (We will discuss audio-visuals in the next session.) Interactivity is the key. As often as possible, let learners work together on a project.

Visuals in the texts. Most religion texts include pictures and other visual aids related to the lesson. Discuss and refer to them as you present the message. Let older learners discuss them in small groups.

Visuals on display. These convey a story or message with a few words and/or pictures. They include posters, murals, collages (images and words overlapping each other), banners (can be made of paper, fabric, a branch, paper bags, embroidered, or made in the form of a kite), large pictures, and signs. Decorate your meeting space to fit the theme in a creative way, using simple, accessible objects.

Boards. Various types of boards can involve learners in more active ways. Felt boards with felt figures can be used to engage learners in a story. Paper "boards" and easels offer the means for drawing pictures and rebuses. Poster boards and bulletin boards can be used to hang pictures or signs that accompany the lesson or story.

Games. Games are excellent for helping learners review, assimilate, and apply a lesson, as long as you do not make them ends in themselves. Some are: crossword puzzles and word searches, rebuses, mazes, board games, relays with objects related to the lesson, Bible (or other faith topic) charades, adaptations of popular TV game shows.

Arts, crafts, experiments. These allow the learners to express their own understanding of the lesson. Some arts and crafts are: drawing; painting; making figures and objects out of paper, modeling clay, papier-mâché, felt, pipe cleaners, fabric, wall paper samples, etc. Learners can make cards for different occasions; dioramas (scenes in a box or other container); a terrarium; candles (under adult supervision only); Advent wreaths or calendars; class or individual scrapbooks. Other activities include making bookmarks with quotes from the Bible or the saints; maps of the Bible lands; timelines and charts. You can have the learners carry out simple science experiments to illustrate a point about the lesson, for example, making sugar crystals to show God's impact on our lives, or having them "analyze" their spiritual DNA.

Puppets. Puppets are an engaging way to let learners retell a story or review a lesson. They can be very simple, such as finger puppets; stick puppets made of construction paper, soft foam board, or paper plates glued to popsicle sticks or dowels; sock puppets with faces drawn on, yarn for hair, and a piece of fabric for clothing.

Drama. Drama assumes many forms and provides a fun way to review and assimilate. Acting out the story, with or without dressing up; doing a dramatic or choral reading; role-playing a situation; and miming (acting without words) are all ways to actively involve the learners. Formulate mystery stories using fictional or real characters and/or situations (for example, what do you think happened to Noah's ark?).

Each of these types of visuals has numerous variations that offer a wide variety of aids to enrich the message you are imparting.

Integrating What You Have Just Learned

■ ***Discuss with your group or reflect on your own: Which media are most effective for learners and why? Write down your reflections and ideas.***

Notes

ON YOUR OWN

■ *Which type of media most strongly conveys a message to you?*

Part Five: Engaging Your Learners

How can you use the symbols and visuals you just read about in a practical way? Some suggestions follow, and you'll certainly discover others. Read this on your own. If you take part in the group sessions, share your reflections with your group.

Primary-age learners

- Pour water from a pitcher into a bowl. Let the children dip their hands in the water. Refer to your text about baptism.
- Have each child draw faces on paper plates and hold them up as you read one of the parables to them, e.g., the Good Samaritan.
- To talk about new life, show the children how to make butterflies out of wallpaper samples and pipe cleaners. Then discuss why the butterfly is a symbol for new life.
- Build a "maze" for the children to go through, using signs with clues, and at the end an object related to your lesson.

In his teaching Jesus made use of "all the resources of interpersonal communication, such as word, silence, metaphor, image, example, and many diverse signs."
GDC 140

Intermediate-age learners

- Invite the children to make a mural or large poster with the symbols linked to the celebration of the Eucharist. Or you could have them work in groups, each group making its own poster.
- Ask the children to each make a shoe box diorama of one of the parables of Jesus.
- Play Bible charades to review a story from the Scripture that was part of your lesson.

For middle-school learners, youth, and high-school learners

- Ask them to each make a banner representing his or her name-saint, including the symbol for the saint. The banner can also illustrate an episode from the life of the saint.
- Have learners form small groups. Assign each group a theme related to a recent lesson, and ask each to compose a word search containing ten words related to that lesson.
- Invite learners to form small groups. Each group is to mime a scene illustrating a virtue or one of the commandments. The others have to guess which sacrament (or virtue or commandment) is being depicted.

For adults or intergenerational gatherings

- Have each family work together (or individuals on their own) to make a family tree. You will need some small tree branches, disposable cups or cans with lids removed, clay, green paper, scissors, glue, and markers.
- Tell a story to the whole gathering (perhaps having different persons reading different parts). Then in the small groups, invite the children to retell the story to the adults, using whatever visuals they choose.
- Go to the internet for free black and white Bible maps you can copy. Choose the map of Palestine at the time of Jesus or the ministry of Jesus. Make a list of the main cities and the events that took place there (give Bible citations). Have the groups find the cities and look up the citations. For example, Bethlehem (Luke 2:1–7); Nazareth (Luke 1:26–27); Cana (John 2:1–2); Capernaum (John 2:12); Sychar (John 4:1–6); Jerusalem (Luke 2:41); Bethany (John 11:1–2); Emmaus (Luke 24:13–14).

As You End This Session

Look for the symbols in your life that have special meaning for you in your relationship with God and with others.

Integrating What You Have Just Learned

- ***Do one of the above activities with your group or on your own. What was the experience like?***
- ***Share with your group any activities you have done that are not mentioned in the above sections. Write down your reflections and ideas.***

Notes

tips

- Instead of just asking verbal questions, appeal to the learners' visual sense.
- Props should be kept as simple as possible.

Community of Love

Litany of Saints

■ ***Begin by closing your eyes and breathing deeply for a few moments as a way of centering yourself. The song for this exercise is a setting of the Litany of Saints. When you feel ready, listen to the song "Litany of Saints" (track 8 on the CD), and imagine yourself in the presence of the holy men and women who've been companions of Jesus. Allow for a few moments of silence at the end.***

■ ***Now listen to the song again, but this time pay special attention to the names, and to any feelings or images that come to mind.***

■ ***Here are the words for you to follow:***

Mary and Joseph, pray for us!
Michael and all angels, pray for us!
John and Zechariah, pray for us!
Anna and Elizabeth, pray for us!

Holy men and women, blessed of the ages,
pray, O pray for us.

Isaac and Jacob, pray for us!
Abraham and Sarah, pray for us!
Miriam and Moses, pray for us!
Jonathan and David, pray for us!

Peter and Andrew, pray for us!
James, John, and Matthew, pray for us!
Phillip and Bartholomew, pray for us!
Stephen and Mathias, pray for us!

Lawrence and Thomas, pray for us!
Dominic and Francis, pray for us!
Helen and Cecelia, pray for us!
Anthony and Benedict, pray for us!

Agnes and Ambrose, pray for us!
Paul, John, and Charles, pray for us!
Judith and Joanna, pray for us!
Bernard and Ignatius, pray for us!

■ ***Write down any reflections in the space porvided so you can recall them later.***

Song Notes

■ *When you're ready, continue by prayerfully reading the following reflection.*

We Don't Walk Alone

When we read the creation story in the book of Genesis, we notice that we were created in God's image and created to live in community. "It is not good for man to be alone," we hear God saying. And so God fashions another, so they might travel through life side by side. From the very beginning we are meant for communion with each other.

As Jesus begins his public ministry he gathers around himself a group of friends to share his hope and dream for the kingdom of God. They travel the roads of Galilee together, sharing both successes and failures. One can easily imagine the many meals they must have shared, the lively discussions about God, and the mutual support they were able to give each other.

Like us, they walked side by side with living saints, holy men and women who were their hope and inspiration. Many times our faith is born from the lives of those around us, extraordinary, but sometimes very ordinary, people who live their lives simply and sincerely in the light of God's grace.

Before his conversion, Ignatius of Loyola was a Spanish aristocrat. He lived the life of a nobleman and a soldier. When his knee was shattered in battle by a cannonball, he was bedridden for many months. In the convent hospital where he recovered, there were only two books: the Bible and a copy of the *Lives of the Saints*. Probably out of sheer boredom he began to read the stories of men and women who had fallen in love with God. He was profoundly changed when reading about the heroic accomplishments of these people because of their belief in Jesus Christ. He was inspired to do something important with his life.

I must abandon myself completely to God.

Blessed Pope John XXIII, *The Journal of a Soul*

Take a few minutes now to reflect on your own life. Think of the men and women, either living or dead, who've inspired you, encouraged you, have been a model for your life as a son or daughter of God. Write down their names and how they've influenced your life.

Notes

What gifts do I have
to offer to others?

■ ***When you're ready, continue reading the reflection that follows.***

The name "saints" has often been used in the history of the Church to address the members of the community. For example, Paul addresses his letter to the "saints who are in Ephesus" or "the saints and faithful brothers and sisters in Christ in Colossae." This seems to reinforce an understanding in the early Church that sainthood and holiness was not something a person earned, but was rather a gift from God bestowed on all the baptized.

We are holy because of our baptism into the Body of Christ. We are brothers and sisters because we have all been marked with the sign of Christ and have become heirs of the glory of his resurrection. While we do not earn our kinship in the Body of Christ, we strive to live in such a way that is authentic to our identity as brothers and sisters. Not only do we receive encouragement, inspiration, and companionship from others, but we offer the same to others. We go out of our way to build up the community of Christ by offering comfort to those in sorrow, hope to those in despair, faith to those who are struggling, visiting those in prison, and caring for the poor among us. This is what we do as family members in the Body of Christ.

We've each been given unique gifts to offer to our brothers and sisters. Sometimes our gifts are apparent and public, such as preaching, singing, teaching, and serving at the eucharistic table. And sometimes the gifts we offer may be hidden and private, like cleaning the church, driving an elderly person to the store, visiting someone in the hospital, or bringing dinner to someone recently widowed.

Take a moment at this point to reflect on what gifts you bring to the Body of Christ. Ask yourself: What can I contribute to the life of the community? How can I build up the family of my church? How have I been blessed by these events? Write down some ideas in the space below.

Notes

■ ***Continue now with the reflection.***

Blessed of the Ages

One of the primary places where the communal life of the Church is expressed is when we gather for worship. We gather on Sunday, the day of resurrection, to celebrate the Eucharist. This word, one we've heard often in our lives, means "to give thanks and praise." It reminds us that our primary purpose when we come together on Sunday is to give God our thanks and praise for the abundant graces and gifts of our lives. When we read the readings we are telling the story of God's faithfulness to us and to our ancestors. We are reminded that God continues to work in our lives and our world. Our hearts are moved with gratitude.

When we celebrate the Eucharist, it's not just us, this parish community that offers our praise and thanks to God. We are also joined by the holy men and women of all times and ages as we unite ourselves with Christ, the Risen One who lifts our prayer of praise to the Father. Throughout all time there is but one Eucharist, one Communion, that Christ offers to God. Every Mass we celebrate, every communion we receive, is part of that one, timeless Eucharist. Our voices are joined with those of our grandparents, great grandparents, all our loved ones, with those of Peter and Andrew, James, Matthew, Mother Teresa, and John XXIII when we gather around the altar on Sunday mornings.

The Time of Prayer

For a few minutes, close your eyes and imagine yourself in God's presence, surrounded by loved ones and holy ones of all the ages. Let yourself stand for awhile in humble reverence before the loving gaze of your God. This is the God who loves you much more than you know. All the ones around you are smiling.

If you'd like to make notes to help you recall your time of prayer, you may do that it the space provided here. During the coming week, you might think of picking up a version of the Lives of the Saints and read about some of the men and women who've gone before us in faith. Let their lives inspire you to live your faith more fully. When you're ready, end with the following prayer, or better, with a prayer in your own words.

God of my heart,
you know me better than I know myself
and you understand that my heart really wants you
to be more a part of my life.
Teach me, Lord, as you would patiently teach a child,
how to allow you to permeate my daily activities.
I don't think I yet comprehend
how much you love me and want to have me close.
Thank you, Lord, from the depths of my heart,
for those who journey with me as brothers and sisters.

When you are ready, end with the Our Father.

The Growing Faith Project booklet for this session is #19

19 People of the Church

Content summary of booklet #19

- ***To proclaim the faith and establish his reign, Christ sends his apostles and their successors. From him they receive the power to act in his home.***
- ***The bishop of the Church of Rome, successor to St. Peter, is "head of the college of bishops, the Vicar of Christ and Pastor of the universal Church on earth."***
- ***Helped by the priests, the deacons, and their coworkers, the bishops authentically teach the faith, celebrate divine worship, and guide their churches as true pastors.***
- ***Lay people share in Christ's priesthood. They live out the grace of baptism and confirmation in all the dimensions of their lives and so fulfill their call to holiness.***

This booklet makes reference to articles 871-945 in the *Catechism of the Catholic Church.*

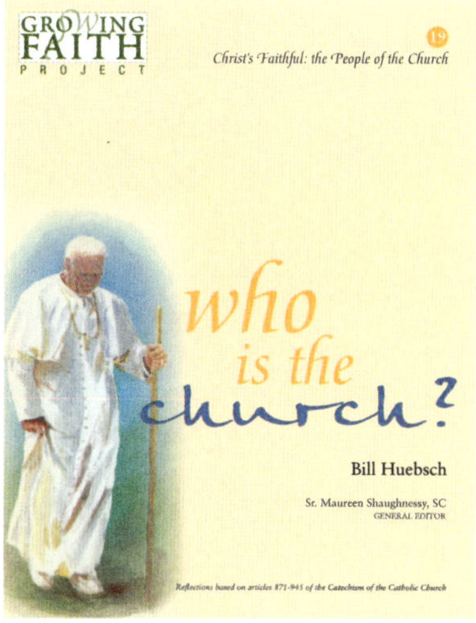

Excerpt from booklet #19

People of God

When we speak of the People of God,
we mean all the Christian faithful,
whether lay, ordained, or in religious life.
All are part of the Church
and each has a certain role to play
in order to build up the community.
All share a common dignity and equality
under Christ,
who reveals Divine Love to us completely.
Hence, diversity of ministry serves the common good.
To bishops who succeed the apostles,
are given the roles of teaching,
sanctifying,
and servant leadership.

Lay people are given a share in the priestly,
prophetic,
and royal office of Christ.

When we use the term "laity" we mean
all the faithful except those in Holy Orders,
that is, the faithful who are committed to Christ
by baptism and the Eucharist,
and who share life in the People of God,
share also in the prophetic,
priestly,
and royal office of Christ.
Lay people share in the ministry of Christ,
in their call to holiness,
their work in teaching,
and their leadership.
They are the front line of the Church.

Lay people share in Christ's priesthood.

Using Technology in Teaching

Goal, Objectives, and Skill

The goal of *Using Technology in Teaching* is to learn when and how to make effective use of technology in your formation sessions.

Your objectives are

- to become familiar with the various means of communication available for catechesis;
- to teach about how the media affect culture;
- to learn strategies for making the most of this technology in and outside of the religion session.

Skill

- Choose and use the most effective forms of technology to communicate the message of Christ to learners.

Preparation

- **Step One:** Experience the material in *Spiritual Exercises* and write your reflections.
- **Step Two:** Read booklet #19 *Who Is the Church?* of the *Growing Faith Project*. Complete the reflections and exercises, recording your reflections.
- **Step Three:** Read the *Tools for Teaching* section carefully. It is important to articulate your reflections and applications in writing or verbally, whether alone or working as part of a group. If you are studying with a group, take advantage of the opportunity to share your experiences in learning sessions.

Connecting Sessions

The previous session provided you with some thoughts and suggestions for using visual aids in your religion session. In this session you will learn how to make effective use of another kind of "visual": the forms of technology.

Part One: Setting the Tone

This optional experience introduces the use of technology in communicating the message of Christ to your learners. Read and reflect on the questions.

Which three television programs do you watch the most? After identifying these, reflect on these questions.

- Do you choose each show based on a) entertainment value; b) moral value; c) educational value; or d) other perceived value (explain) of the program? Which of these values ranked the highest as the reason for watching each program?
- What does this tell you about your TV viewing habits?

> The media has become essential for evangelization and catechesis.
>
> GDC 160

Part Two: Importance of This Session

This section presents the importance of understanding and using communication media. Read this on your own. If you take part in the group sessions, share your reflections with your group.

How can you make the means of communication an effective part of your catechesis?

- Become familiar with the various forms of technology available for catechesis.
- Teach about how the media affects culture.
- Learn strategies for making the most of the means of communication in and outside of the religion session.

Take a moment to ask yourself: has my sense of responsibility in the use of these media grown with the same leaps and bounds as the development of the various forms of technology? Do they really contribute to the betterment of society or are some of them just the result of a consumer mentality?

Communication media can be a powerful force for good: in providing quick, accurate information, depicting values, fostering understanding and assistance among nations, sharing discoveries, and promoting education, as well as offering entertainment. But there is a dark side to communication media and its power.

As catechists and teachers we need to learn how to use these media in our programs and to educate learners about how to use them to become better persons and followers of Christ. Media literacy is essential to help learners become discerning viewers, listeners, and users of the media. We will speak out and take action when the media promote ideas and practices and ways of life that are counter to the commandments and the teachings of Christ.

Integrating What You Have Just Learned

- ***Discuss with your group or reflect on your own: How have the media influenced—positively or negatively—the faith of the learners? What are the values they have learned (or not learned)? Write down your reflections and ideas.***

Notes

tips

- Decide which communication media are most effective for your learners and your lesson.
- Know how to use the equipment and test it ahead of time.

ON YOUR OWN

- *Fold a sheet of paper in half lengthwise. In one column list the positive aspects of the media that you yourself have experienced. In the other list the negative. Reflect on these aspects. How can you build on the positive and offset or remove the negative in your home?*

Part Three: The Means of Communication

The means of communication vary in purpose, effect, and use. Study this brief presentation of those that can be effectively employed in and outside of religion sessions. Read this on your own. If you take part in the group sessions, share your reflections with your group.

- **VHS tapes and DVDs.** Clips from popular films and TV programs can emphasize and illustrate themes of a lesson, either as an introduction or to assist assimilation. They can also be used to illustrate the influence they have on our culture and thinking.

- **Music cassettes and CDs.** Soft instrumental music can be used as background for prayer experiences. Music for young children is an excellent way to involve them in a lesson theme, especially if you use gestures or dance with it. For older children and youth, you can use some popular music to spark discussions on related themes or topics. Again, songs can be used to illustrate the influence they have on our culture and thinking.

- **Radio, iPods, MP3s, and cell phones.** While used more on an individual basis, you can discuss the use of these means, especially in connection with games and music. iPods also allow the owners to view movies as well as information.

- **Television.** Although television programs generally cannot be used during the religion session, you can still make them part of your lesson or refer to them during a discussion. Educational programs often have information or programming that may be referred to in your lesson, for example in relation to creation, people, history, and so on. How and why do certain programs or characters become cultural icons?

- **Computers.** One aspect of computers is their use as tools for creative activities. In addition, a world of information, formation, and fun is at your fingertips on the internet. The internet has many websites with downloadable activities. Other websites offer facts on poverty, missions, ecology, the saints, and so much more. Visit www.intothefields.org for material and links related to such programs.

  You can also use the computer to keep in touch with other catechists and teachers by means of email, chat rooms, bulletin boards, and similar forums. Online courses and degree programs are widely available, including courses from Catholic universities.

- **CD-ROMs.** CD-ROM technology is another tool for learning, including software that provides libraries and learning paths for every age level, on a variety of subjects.

- **Computer and video games.** Varying widely in content, from educational and fun games for children to violent games for adults, video games now include more Christian games; for example, *Catechumen* and Bible-based games.

Each of these media has its own "language" which Catholic educators need to learn in order to present Christ's message to the people of today.

Integrating What You Have Just Learned

- ***Discuss as a group or reflect on your own: Which of the above media have you used in your religion sessions, and how? How successful was your lesson? Write down your ideas and reflections.***

Notes

Part Four: The Media Affect Our Culture

For better or worse the media do affect our culture. As a catechist or teacher you need to reflect on the impact of media, and share this with learners in age-appropriate ways. Read this on your own. If you take part in the group sessions, share your reflections with your group.

In the *Decree on the Means of Social Communication*, the Second Vatican Council spoke clearly about forming consciences especially with regard to three issues: information, the rights of art and the moral law, and the representation of good and evil.[1] Precisely in these areas the media have had a powerful impact on our culture.

- **Information.** How many people question the news as it is presented on the television and radio—particularly on TV, with the immediacy of its images and super-speed reporting? It is not always easy to remember that media outlets are very particular and completely selective in choosing the information they provide, as well as the manner in which they provide it. "Reality, for many, is what the media recognizes as real; what the media do not acknowledge seems of little importance."[2] For example, how do the media present the plight of the poor and marginalized? What part do they play in the consumerism and materialism of our time? How are the teachings of the Church presented in the secular media? How do the media affect politics, economics, and education? How aware are we of media ownership and its increasing concentration in the hands of a small group of multi-national conglomerates? If there are less than ten real media owners in the world, how many perspectives are really available to us as we seek to inform ourselves.

- **The rights of art and the moral law.** What values (or non-values) do children, youth, and adults learn from their favorite TV, film, or computer/video game characters? What challenges do they face, and how do they face them?

Integrating What You Have Just Learned

- ***Choose a popular TV program (news or entertainment) and analyze it as a group or on your own, using the issues noted above. How would you as a Catholic rate the program and why? Write down your reflections and ideas.***

Notes

[1] *Decree on the Means of Social Communication (Communio et Progressio)*, nos 5–7

[2] Aetatis Novae, *On the Twentieth Anniversary of* Communio et Progressio, no. 4

Part Five: Making the Most of the Media

In this section we will look at some strategies for using the media in your formation sessions and helping learners be discerning in their use of the media. Read this on your own. If you take part in the group sessions, share your reflections with your group.

Strategies for Different Age Levels

Primary-age children

- Ask children who their favorite TV characters are. Ask each of them to act out something their character does (a song, a phrase, a story), and to explain why they like that character.
- If you teach a lesson on forgiveness, use a video story to emphasize the theme.
- Use excerpts from a movie about friendship and compare the types of friendship by having the children draw pictures of the characters, or sing the songs.
- Have the children use the internet to find pages for their age level on different topics. Visit www.intothefields.org for material and links.

For intermediate-age learners

- Ask learners to think about their favorite video or computer game (if they don't have one, they can choose a movie). Who is the hero or heroine? What challenge does he/she face? How does he/she overcome it?
- Invite learners to work in small groups. Each group should choose a popular song, draw colors to go with it, then write down the actual words. Have each group talk about what the song says and its message. Why did they choose the color(s) they used?
- Have the children work in small groups of two or more to prepare a report about an event or happening in their school, neighborhood, or parish. After they present their reports, discuss their experience.

> Catechists must seriously commit themselves to learning how to use these media to bring people to Christ.
> NDC 30

Middle-school learners, youth, high school learners, or adults

- Ask learners to keep a record of the television programs they watch over the course of a week. For at least one of the programs have them answer questions such as the following: Who are the main characters? What values do you learn from them? How would you rate this program as to its portrayal of Christian values and why? Invite them to share some of their findings.

- Arrange a panel discussion on the topic: When should the public's right to information give way to an individual's right to privacy?

- Invite learners to form small groups and role-play a situation from one of the television programs or movies they have watched recently. Then ask them to role-play it again, this time with a "Christian twist." What are the differences, if any?

- Ask learners to form small groups and come up with an idea for a Christian record, computer game, TV program, whatever means they choose. Each group will then present their ideas to the larger group for feedback.

As You End This Session

Reflect on how the media have influenced your life (for example, choices in clothes, political views, desire for more things, language, attitudes toward other people.

Integrating What You Have Just Learned

- ***Look at the suggested strategies for the age level of the learners you teach. Discuss in a group or reflect on your own: what is the purpose of each activity, that is, what do you want the learners to come away with? Write down your ideas and reflections.***

Notes

tips

- Preview all materials you will be using with your learners. "Forward" any videos, DVDs, CDs, etc., to the sections you want to use beforehand.
- Remember, the media are resources to assist you in teaching a lesson. They are not an end in themselves.

Recognizing God's Voice

Holy Darkness

■ ***Find a quiet place where you won't be disturbed. Most people find it easier to center and focus if they close their eyes and take deep, slow breaths. As you inhale, imagine that God is filling you with peace and joy. As you exhale, imagine that you are letting go of all anxiety and stress. Continue for a couple minutes as you sit in God's holy presence.***

■ ***The grace we ask for in this exercise is to be able to discern and recognize God's voice in our lives. Begin by listening to the song "Holy Darkness" (track 9 on the CD). Without trying to understand its meaning, let the music surround you and speak to your heart. Allow for a moment of quiet at the end.***

Then listen again, but this time pay more attention to the words that are sung. If there are any words, images, or feelings that surface as you listen, make note of these. If you find yourself distracted or resistant, be aware of this as well.

■ ***Here are the words for you to follow:***

Holy darkness, blessed night,
heaven's answer hidden from our sight.
As we await you, O God of silence,
we embrace your holy night.

I have tried you in fires of affliction;
I have taught your soul to grieve.
In the barren soil of your loneliness
there I will plant my seed.

I have taught you the price of compassion;
you have stood before the grave.
Though my love can seem like a raging storm,
this is the love that saves.

In your deepest hour of darkness
I will give you wealth untold.
When the silence stills your spirit,
will my riches fill your soul.

■ ***Write down your thoughts and reflections in the space provided here.***

Song Notes

When you're ready, continue by slowly reading the following reflection.

Spiritual Attentiveness

The spirituality of St. Ignatius of Loyola that inspired these exercises is rooted in the mystery of the Incarnation. The mystery of God taking human flesh was not just a matter of his becoming a man in the person of Jesus of Nazareth. Much more than that, in the mind of Ignatius, the divine presence permeates all reality—every creature, every human person, every event, every hope and desire, every joy and sorrow, and finally, even death itself. At every moment of our life God is there in love and blessing.

The challenge for us who strive to walk in God's presence is how to recognize the voice of God in the midst of all the other voices. This is important if we are sincere about our desire to follow God's gentle inspiration in our lives and to be companions of Jesus in his mission. We're speaking here, of course, about those subtle, quiet internal voices that each of us "feels" when we are attentive. What does God's voice feel like? How do we distinguish the voice of God from other voices? How do we know which inspiration comes from God and which comes from the Evil One?

Discerning God's voice in our lives first requires attentiveness. The practice of the "examination of conscience" described in Session 16 is a very effective way of paying attention to God's working in our daily lives. This is why this ritual was considered by Ignatius to be such an important spiritual practice for a person seeking union with God.

When silence
stills your spirit,
riches will
fill your soul.

Take a moment to reflect on your personal use of the practice of the examen. Have you been able to incorporate it into the ritual of your day? Have you found it helpful? Is there something you need to do to make it a more "natural" part of your daily routine? Write down your reflections here.

Notes

■ ***Continue reading the reflection.***

Consolation and Desolation

As we get to know someone, we become familiar with the ways they communicate, their tone of voice, their subtle non-verbal cues, and more than anything, we begin to know their heart. The same is true in our relationship with God. As we spend time in prayer, we learn to recognize the inner voice of God. We can learn to discern God's voice by the way he communicates with us.

Discernment involves recognizing the interplay of consolation and desolation in our spiritual lives. If we make a list of the fruits of the spirit—charity, joy, peace, patience, kindness, goodness, faithfulness, gentleness—we'd have a good description of what "consolation" feels like. Ignatius defines consolation as every increase in faith, hope, and love, a feeling of interior joy that attracts us to God by filling us with peace and quiet joy. On the other hand, Ignatius defines desolation as entirely the opposite of consolation: darkness of soul, turmoil of spirit, an inclination to what is sinful and unhealthy, a feeling of restlessness that leads to a disturbance of our faith, a sense of hopelessness, and a lack of love.

Where and how do I recognize God's voice?

Perhaps you'll notice that the words used here are feeling words. While we don't usually make decisions based on feelings, when we're talking of discernment, listening to our feelings is the key to recognizing God's voice in our lives. Feelings may be precarious to understand, but we must learn to discern them, because it is through feelings that we come to know how God speaks to us.

A practical example might help to clarify the interplay of consolation and desolation. Imagine that we're going through our day, perhaps even a difficult day, but with an inner consolation; our heart is peaceful and we're grateful for God's goodness to us. And then we get a phone call from our pastor inviting us to be on the parish council. As we weigh the question over the next few days, we realize that when we imagine ourselves sitting on the council we feel anxious, agitated, and gloomy. These feelings of "desolation" are a pretty good indication that being on the parish council is not a good idea at this point in our lives.

Take a moment to reflect on the interplay of consolation and desolation in your life. You may not be very experienced at paying attention to these movements of the spirit. Can you begin to recognize times of consolation? Of desolation? Write your thoughts below.

Notes

Where Have You Gone, Lord?

Desolation is never from God, although God allows us to experience it at times. The Evil Spirit will always try to discourage us, causing us to feel spiritual turmoil, hoping to lure us away from the path of grace and holiness. Sometimes God will allow us to feel spiritual dryness, emptiness, barrenness so that we might experience our dependence on God. Even long periods of desolation in our prayer life can be God's way of emptying our souls of pride and arrogance so that we may recognize that consolation is God's gift and nothing we can earn or create on our own.

Ignatius encourages us to remember and hold on to times of great consolation when God seems so close and we feel that great inner joy and peace that comes from being with the One who loves us. When we experience times of spiritual dryness, Ignatius encourages us to recall those experiences of consolation and to draw strength from them. The Enemy will always try to discourage us, to make us wonder if God has abandoned us, to tempt us to lose hope. If we remember those times of great consolation, we can draw comfort and hope from them even in the midst of our desolation.

The Time of Prayer

Close your eyes now and allow yourself to rest for a moment in the quiet, peaceful presence of the God who loves you more than you can imagine. This is the God who wants to be close to you and to share his heart with you.

When you're ready, speak to God with the following prayer, or better, with your own words.

This is a good time to make some notes about your experience of this exercise. What did you learn? What was helpful? What was not? What was confusing? What would you like to learn more about? During the coming week, play the song "Holy Darkness" often to remind yourself of this reflection.

Great and wonderful God,
I stand before you as your humble servant,
wanting to hear your voice and needing your help to guide my life.
Grant me the grace, Lord,
to discern the movement of your Spirit in my life,
to recognize when it is you speaking in my life
and when it is the Evil Spirit.
I want to follow your path for me,
to be generous with my heart
and to bring the good news of your love to those I teach.

When you are ready, end with the Our Father.

The Growing Faith Project booklets for this session are #23 and #24

23 Baptism

Content summary of booklet #23

- ***Christian initiation is accomplished in three sacraments: baptism, confirmation, and the Eucharist.***
- ***Baptism consists in immersing the candidates in water, or pouring it on their heads, while invoking the Father, Son, and Holy Spirit.***
- ***Martyrs, catechumens, and those who seek God sincerely can be saved even without baptism.***
- ***Baptism is a grace and a gift of God.***

This booklet makes reference to articles 1212-1284 in the *Catechism of the Catholic Church.*

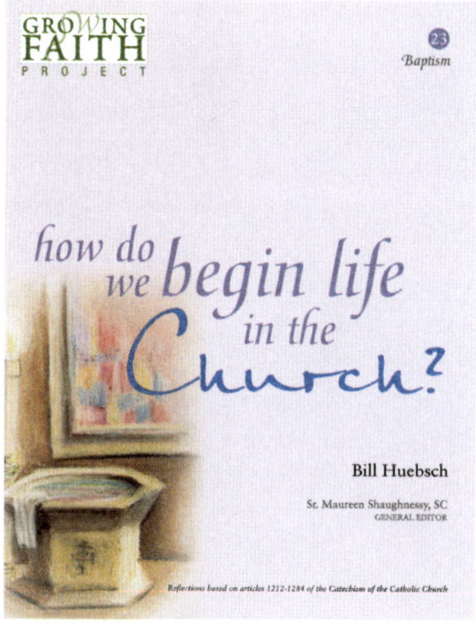

24 Confirmation

Content summary of booklet #24

- ***Confirmation perfects baptismal grace. Through the Holy Spirit this sacrament joins us more closely to Christ and the Church, and helps us witness to the Christian faith.***
- ***Candidates for confirmation must profess the faith, be in the state of grace, and desire to receive the sacrament.***
- ***In confirmation the person is anointed with sacred chrism; the minister lays his hands on the person's head with the words: "Be sealed with the Gift of the Holy Spirit."***

This booklet makes reference to articles 1285-1321 in the *Catechism of the Catholic Church.*

Excerpt from booklet #23

Initiation

The term comes to us from a Greek word
which means, literally,
to plunge or immerse.
Going into the water is a symbol of entry
into Christ's death,
and coming out of it a "new person"
is a symbol of the resurrection.
In the early Church, it was also called
"the water of rebirth" or
"the washing of rebirth"
in the Letter to Titus,
chapter 3, verse 5.

It has also been called "enlightenment"
because by it, we enter the community
in which grace and light are received and shared.
Indeed, through baptism, we ourselves become
light for the world.

Baptism
is birth into the
new life
of love.

Teaching about Christian Initiation

Goal, Objectives, and Skill

The goal of *Teaching about Christian Initiation* is to explore with learners the nature of Christian initiation.

Your objectives are

- to reflect on what initiation means;
- to teach learners about the lifelong journey of initiation and faith;
- to teach learners about the sacraments of initiation.

Skill

- Help learners continue their faith journey, especially by making that journey yourself.

Preparation

- **Step One:** Experience the material in *Spiritual Exercises* and write your reflections.
- **Step Two:** Read booklets *#23 How Do We Begin Life in the Church?* and *#24 How Does the Holy Spirit Strengthen Us?* of the *Growing Faith Project*. Complete the reflections and exercises, recording your reflections.
- **Step Three:** Read the *Tools for Teaching* section carefully. It is important to articulate your reflections and applications in writing or verbally, whether alone or working as part of a group. If you are studying with a group, take advantage of the opportunity to share your experiences in learning sessions.

Connecting Sessions

After learning how to use various ways of teaching a lesson, you will be able to practice them as you prepare to teach learners about Christian initiation.

Part One: Setting the Tone

This optional story introduces you to Christian initiation as the beginning of the Christian's journey of faith. Read and reflect on your own.

An old legend tells of a powerful man who promised a young woman a gift of rare value if she would go through a field of corn and select the largest and ripest ear. In doing so she was not to pause or go backward or wander here and there. The value of the gift was to be in proportion to the size and perfection of the ear. The young woman passed by many fine ears of corn, but was so anxious to get the largest and most perfect that she kept on without plucking any. As she continued, the ears began to grow smaller and smaller, until finally they were so stunted that she was ashamed to pick any. Since she was not allowed to go backward, she came out on the other side without any. For lack of decision she missed the very gift she coveted.[1]

> Adhering to Jesus Christ
> sets in motion a process
> of continuing conversion,
> which lasts for the whole of life.
> GDC 56

[1] Anthony Castle, *A Treasury of Quips, Quotes and Anecdotes*, Twenty-Third Publications

Part Two: Importance of This Session

This section presents the importance of making the journey of faith with your learners. Read this on your own. If you take part in the group sessions, share your reflections with the group.

Explore with the learners the nature of Christian initiation.

- Reflect on what initiation means.
- Teach learners about the lifelong journey of initiation and faith.
- Teach learners about the sacraments of initiation.

The Lord of the Rings, the classic by J.R.R. Tolkien, is above all about a journey, a journey that may be compared to that of Jesus and to the journey of St. Augustine, which he describes in his *Confessions*. The journey of the ring bearer, and that of his friends, is a "journey of the heart." Frodo makes a free choice to carry the ring to Mount Doom in order to destroy it, even though he does "not know the way."

None of the members of the Fellowship, in fact—not even Gandalf—truly knows the way. As the battle continues—to save Middle Earth from Sauron—their journeys take them on unforeseen paths.

The faith journey each of us makes also takes us along unforeseen paths. We each have our own burdens to carry, our own mission to complete, our own lessons to learn. But as catechists and teachers you are also invited to be companions to learners on their journey. The journey, which began with the gift of life from God, does not end until our return to God.

Integrating What You Have Just Learned

- ***Discuss with your group—or reflect on—some of the unforeseen events or paths that have been part of your faith journey. How have these affected your growth in faith? How can you use these experiences in your mission as a catechist or teacher? Write down your reflections and ideas.***

Notes

ON YOUR OWN

- *Who has been most influential in your journey of faith? Explain.*

Part Three: Reflections on Initiation

Christian initiation, unlike initiation into many other groups, has a lasting effect on our lives. Read this on your own. If you take part in the group sessions, share your reflections with the group.

Catechesis is an essential element of the process of Christian initiation. For catechumens, catechesis both precedes and follows baptism. For those baptized as infants, catechesis follows baptism and nurtures the baptized in fulfillment of initiation in the celebration of confirmation and Eucharist. Beyond initiation, we are increasingly aware that growing in discipleship with Christ is a lifelong process. In this process of initiation and growing in discipleship, we can identify some distinct experiences characteristic of the journey of faith for believers.

- **The experience of encountering Jesus through the gospels.** Initiation requires a comprehensive formation that is more than just learning the truths of faith. Catechesis for initiation nurtures a personal relationship with the Christ of the gospels through conversion of life, so that the Christian lives his or her baptism and so enters more deeply into the mystery of Christ.
- **The experience of community.** Through initiation the person becomes a part of the Church community and, with the community, learns to live and celebrate the faith, share it with others, and serve his or her sisters and brothers.
- **The experience of ritual and celebration.** In the parish community learners experience ritual and symbols, which are linked to their life as much as possible. They learn to turn to God in prayer, individually and with others.
- **The experience of companionship.** Christian companionship is also important for sharing and guidance in living the faith. Depending on the age and situation of the learner, the companion might be a member of the family, a friend, a catechist or teacher, or another adult leader or mentor.
- **The Christian experience of time.** With the faith community and in their personal lives, learners also have a Christian experience of time, both in the unfolding of the liturgical year and the sacraments, as well as in the unfolding of their own story as part of salvation history.

ON YOUR OWN

Which two of the experiences on this page do you feel is most important to you on your spiritual journey and why?

Integrating What You Have Just Learned

Share with your group or reflect on your own: In what ways are the five experiences key to the journey of Christian initiation? Write your reflections and ideas below.

Notes

Part Four: Making the Journey

Share with learners the idea of our lifelong journey as Christians. Read this on your own. If you take part in the group sessions, share your reflections with your group.

Strategies for Different Age Levels

Primary-age children

- With primary-age learners you can make or acquire a simple poster showing our journey during the liturgical year. If you teach first and second graders, talk about only one season at a time; gradually they will experience the connection.

- Sing songs about the journey and about community, suited to their age level.

- Play musical chairs but replace the music with a list of words related to your theme. When you say the key word (e.g., "Jesus" or "gospel"), the children sit down.

- Pray together for families in the parish, country, and world.

Intermediate-age learners

- Prepare a picture of a tree. Have the children work in small groups and write on index cards important elements of our growth in faith. Mix all the cards up, then ask the children to match each one to a tree part (foundational elements at roots, etc.).

- Have the children sit in a circle and ask each child to take off one shoe and put it in the center. Each is then to choose a shoe not his or her own. Talk about trying to walk in another person's shoes, then about walking in the shoes of Jesus.

- Ask the children to work in groups and prepare a simple prayer based on a certain object or symbol representing a journey, for example, a walking stick, a bag, a road, and so on.

Middle-school learners, youth, high-school learners, adults, and intergenerational gatherings

- Prepare a "Christian Survivors' Journey" in which learners go from one table or desk to another, gathering information or acquiring objects they need for their lifelong journey.

- Let them experience a simple prayer labyrinth (representing a journey) in which you set up a circular path (using rug samples or heavy pieces of paper) that narrows as it goes toward the center.

- If possible, arrange a visit to a nearby shrine or a church other than the parish church. The visit will be in the form of a pilgrimage, with a brief tour and prayers said at the site.

Integrating What You Have Just Learned

- ***Discuss or reflect on your own: What means have you used or would you use to teach learners about Christian initiation? Explain. Write down your reflections and ideas.***

Notes

ON YOUR OWN

- *What other images besides "journey" do you or would you use to describe your lifelong conversion to Christ? Why?*

Part Five: Connecting the Sacraments of Initiation

Catechesis for initiation is closely linked to the sacraments of Christian initiation. Read this section on your own. If you take part in the group sessions, share your reflections with your group.

The sacraments of baptism and confirmation are intimately connected to one another, as they are to the Eucharist. All three are sacraments of initiation, and the omission of one makes a person's Christian initiation incomplete. Yet, in the Latin rite, while catechumens celebrate all three sacraments at the Easter Vigil, Catholics baptized at birth don't celebrate the other sacraments of initiation until several years later. Because of this, children and youth, as well as adults, do not experience the relationship between the three sacraments in the same way as catechumens.

Intentionally engaging learners in age-appropriate ways will benefit the learners as they come to understand the relationship between a sacramental life and their own lives.

Strategies for Different Age Levels

Primary-age learners

Again, learners this age work with concrete concepts. The youngest are just beginning to link concepts together. Activities need to be concrete and, for the most part, involve body movement.

- Have the children put together baptism-confirmation "kits," with paper cutouts of each of the following: a white baptismal garment, a candle, a shell (used to baptize), a small container of oil, a picture or cutout of a dove.
- Emphasize that we are able to receive Jesus in the Eucharist because we are baptized into the Church community. Sing a song that makes the connection.
- Bless the children with water, then have a "meal" (snack) together and pray for those who are hungry.
- Choose two pictures illustrating a baptism, enlarge them, make a black border around the enlarged copies, then cut them into puzzle pieces. Have the children work in two teams to put the puzzle pieces together one by one on a larger sheet of paper. (You might want to draw in the outlines of the pieces to make it easier.)

Intermediate-age learners

At this age level, learners tend to have a more developed ability to link concepts and to engage in projects that are more involved. If you have a computer, some of these activities may be done, at least partly, on the computer.

- Invite each child to make a personalized stained glass window with his or her name and the symbols of baptism and confirmation.
- Have learners renew their baptismal promises in a prayer service.
- Ask learners to do a "shoebox project" and call it "My Christian Initiation." They can use index cards with photos, drawings, symbols, or their own writing to describe each of the sacraments, the rituals, the meaning, their experience (whatever they can recall).
- Invite them to work together to make a calendar with their own photos and the dates of their baptism and First Eucharist.
- Have the children write a "gospel," which will tell others how they met Jesus, came to know Jesus better, and how Jesus is part of their lives. The "gospel" can be illustrated, copied, and put together.

Catechists should teach "that Baptism is the foundation of the Christian life...[and] that Confirmation increases and deepens the grace of Baptism.

NDC 36A.1–2

Middle-school learners, youth, high-school learners, adults, and intergenerational gatherings

These learners are more capable of abstract thinking and complex projects.

- Invite middle-school learners, youth, or participants of intergenerational gatherings to make their own scrapbooks with the theme "My Christian Initiation." At this level, learners tend to have developed a more attuned capacity to communicate their own thoughts in their work.
- After discussing the symbols for baptism and/or confirmation, have learners work in groups and come up with at least three symbols of their own, along with the explanation for their choices.
- Divide the learners into groups and ask the members of each group to interview each other about their experience—both past and present—of the sacraments. Have them articulate how the sacraments affect their lives. Ask them to summarize the main points that emerge and share them with the larger group.
- Celebrate the dates of their baptism and First Eucharist by making a video using old photos.

As You End This Session

- Decide on two practical ways the effects of Christian initiation can have a greater impact on your own life and your teaching mission, and take action.

Integrating What You Have Just Learned

- ***Discuss in your group or reflect on your own: How would you (or how do you) explain the connection between the sacraments of initiation to learners? What images, activities, and words seem the most helpful? Write down your reflections and ideas.***

Notes

Love One Another

Grace Upon Grace

In this twentieth exercise, the last in this second year of reflections, we'll look back on where we've been since we began this journey of faith. This will provide an opportunity to treasure the grace that God has given us. St. Ignatius, in crafting his Spiritual Exercises, understood how important it is for a person not to move ahead without stopping occasionally to look back and draw spiritual nourishment from the consolation God has given. Ignatius calls this looking back a "repetition." And so, rather than providing new material, this exercise invites you to read the spiritual journal you've been keeping in order to savor those powerful moments of grace, to relish them, and find even more goodness in them.

Share the grace of your spiritual journey.

For some, this exercise might be a challenge and feel unsettling. Why waste our time by going over what we've already done? We're so conditioned by our culture to keep moving ahead and not waste time. In the life of the Spirit, however, remaining with any grace or consolation that's been given to us is never a waste of time. It's a way to nourish that deep-down hunger we prayed about in our very first exercise.

First, prepare yourself by closing your eyes and breathing slowly and deeply for a few moments. As you feel yourself relax, take time to rest in the presence of the God who loves you.

The next step is to look back at what you've written in the first and second sessions of these exercises. Pay special attention to the notes you made at the very end of each exercise. This is where you tried to put into words the special goodness of that exercise for you, to name what you learned and how God drew your soul in prayer. In the presence of God read through what you wrote, remembering and allowing yourself time to be grateful for what you've experienced. Then, after you've reviewed your notes, make a list on the next page of the graces that seem most significant to you.

Notes

When you've finished, look back over what you've written. These are the things that you should spend more time with. For now, pick just one or two of them. Remember back to that moment in the previous exercise and recall what it felt like. What was so significant about it? Why does it mean so much to you? Embrace it and savor it. You shouldn't feel compelled to rush forward. Even if you spend all the remaining time with these one or two graces, give yourself the opportunity to rest in God's infinite love and mercy. There's no need to figure anything out or draw a conclusion. Just be with God in the moment. Spend anywhere from ten to thirty minutes here before moving on.

■ ***When you're ready, continue with the following reflection.***

All the World Will Know

It's helpful at this point to remind ourselves that whenever God gives us a consoling grace, it's not for us to hold and keep for ourselves. Graces are given to us to share—to bring light, peace, joy, and hope to others. The grace that we've been given is a grace that's meant to be given away so that it may become grace for someone else.

Take a moment to reflect on how you might share the grace of this spiritual journey with someone else, perhaps a spouse, a parent, a son or daughter, another catechist, or a teacher. Or maybe there'd be an opportunity to gather as a group with other teachers and catechists to tell each other how these exercises have affected your life, what's been helpful and what's been hard. Write down some ways you can share the gift of these exercises with others.

Notes

Above all, maintain constant love for one another, for love coveres a multitude of sins. Be hospitable to one another without complaining. Like good stewards of the manifold grace of God, serve one another with whatever gift each of you has received. Whoever speaks must do so as one speaking the very words of God; whoever serves must do so with the strength that God supplies, so that God may be glorified in all things through Jesus Christ. To him belong the glory and the power for ever and ever. Amen.
(1 Peter 4:8–11)

Love shows itself
in humble service.

Servants of All

If we read the account of the Last Supper in John's gospel, there's a very moving passage where Jesus is teaching us, his disciples, the most important things we need to remember when he is taken from our sight. This is his farewell address to us, his final instructions. With very poignant words, Jesus tells us he will abide in us, just as God, his Father, abides in him. He goes on to say that if we keep his commandments we will abide in his love. Then he spells out for us the one most important commandment: we should love each other as he has loved us. He doesn't just tell us to love each other, but to love as he himself has loved.

It's probably not a mistake that Jesus' farewell address is positioned in John's gospel immediately after the story about washing the disciples' feet. We might easily imagine Jesus saying to us, "If you want to understand what I mean by loving each other as I've loved you, remember what I just did. Do for each other what I have done." We know all too well that Jesus took upon himself the humble role of the household servant by wrapping a towel around his waist and kneeling to wash his disciples' feet. In other words, he teaches us that the way we show our love is by becoming servants. He gave us an example in which he's very clear that the service of love is not about having a magnetic personality, or being a gifted teacher, or having the financial resources to support each other. Love shows itself in humble service, taking on those roles that no one else wants and being willing to get dirty knees.

■ ***Listen to the song "As I Have Done for You" (track 10 on the CD) now. Its lyrics echo many of the themes and graces of these reflections we've done. Allow the music to remind you of all the graces God has bestowed on you in these exercises.***

■ ***Here are the words for you to follow:***

I, your Lord and Master,
now become your servant.
I who made the moon and stars
will kneel to wash your feet.
This is my commandment:
love as I have loved you.
Kneel to wash each other's feet
as I have done for you.

All the world will know you are my disciples
By the love that you offer,
the kindness you show.
You have heard the voice of God
in the words that I have spoken.
You beheld heaven's glory
and have seen the face of God.

I must leave you now only for a moment.
I must go to my Father to make you a home.
On the day of my return
I will come to take you with me
To the place I have promised
where your joy will have no end.

"As I Have Done for You" by Dan Schutte. From the collection **Glory in the Cross**, ©2001, Daniel L. Schutte. Published by OCP Publications, 5536 NE Hassalo, Portland, OR 97213.

Song Notes

The Time of Prayer

Close your eyes and imagine Jesus' face before you. Imagine looking into his eyes and allowing him to look back into yours. As he looks into your heart, imagine him smiling with pride and delight in you. You are his beloved.

End with the following prayer, or better, with a prayer in your own words.

The final part of this exercise is something that you'll take with you during the coming week. Go back and look at the list of graces and memories you made at the beginning of this exercise. Find a place in your home to put that list so you'll be reminded of it during your daily activities. When you wake up, go to bed, drive, or make dinner, let these graces follow you and fill you with gratitude.

Great and generous Jesus, Lord of my life,
as I've looked back over the weeks of my journey with you
my heart is overwhelmed with gratitude.
Sometimes the steps you've taken with me are so small
that I hardly notice that we're moving on.
But when I look back I can see the distance we've come
and how you've always been there at my side.
I pray that you help me be a good teacher,
using the consoling graces you've given me
to offer light, hope, and peace to those who need it.

When you are ready, end with the Our Father.

The Growing Faith Project booklets for this session are #28 and #29

28 Holy Orders

Content summary of booklet #28

- *The whole Church is a priestly people. Through baptism all the faithful share in the priesthood of Christ, called the "common priesthood of the faithful."*
- *The ministerial priesthood differs in essence because it confers a sacred power for the service of the faithful, exercised by teaching, divine worship, and pastoral governance.*
- *Since the beginning, the ordained ministry has been conferred and exercised in three degrees: that of bishops, that of priests, and that of deacons.*
- *The sacrament of holy orders is celebrated by the laying on of hands, followed by a solemn prayer of consecration.*

This booklet makes reference to articles 1533–1600 in the *Catechism of the Catholic Church.*

29 Matrimony

Content summary of booklet #29

- *Marriage is based on the will of a man and woman to give themselves, each to the other, mutually and definitively, in order to live a covenant of faithful and fruitful love.*
- *Unity, permanence, and openness to fertility are essential to marriage.*
- *The Christian home is the place where children receive their first proclamation of the faith. For this reason the family home is rightly called "the domestic Church," a community of grace and prayer, a school of human virtues and of Christian charity.*

This booklet makes reference to articles 1601–1666 in the *Catechism of the Catholic Church.*

Excerpt from booklet #28

We are made for service

Holy Orders is a gift of the Spirit to the Church,
continuing the mission of Christ
in unique and important roles.
There are three levels of these roles,
each receiving Holy Orders:
bishop,
priest,
deacon.
Incorporation into the order of bishop,
priest, or deacon
was accomplished by a special rite
called, of course, "ordination."
This is a liturgical and sacramental action,
a public action in the Church
which confers the gift of the Holy Spirit.
This gift is one of love and service.
The power or energy of love
is a sacred power.
The visible sign of this sacrament
is the laying on of hands by a bishop.

All the faithful share in the priesthood of Christ.

Summing Up

Goal

The goal of *Summing Up* is to review and integrate everything you have studied in sessions eleven to nineteen of *Tools for Teaching*.

Preparation

- **Step One:** Experience the material in *Spiritual Exercises* and write your reflections.
- **Step Two:** Read booklets #28 *How Does God Consecrate for the Service of the Church?* and #29 *How Is Love Blessed and Celebrated?* of the *Growing Faith Project*. Do the reflections and exercises, recording your reflections.
- **Step Three:** Review sessions eleven to nineteen and complete the exercises in the Review section.

Part One: How to Sum Up

The aim of this session is to help you review and integrate all the material of the preceding nine sessions.

To help you review each session

- Make sure you study the Goal, Objectives, and the Skill first.
- Read the notes you made for each section of *Integrating What You Have Just Learned*. These will help you call to mind the purpose of each session, and what you took away from it.
- As you review the actual content of the session, give more attention to the body of the content than to the strategies. If you have not already done so, highlight important or key phrases or ideas.

Part Two: Review the Goal, Objectives, and Skill of Sessions Eleven to Fourteen

Let these guide you in your review, as they are the main ideas, skills, and attitudes you took with you from these sessions. Read on your own or study with others.

Session Eleven: Teaching within the Whole Community

The goal was to help you learn how to involve learners in the life of the community.

Your objectives were

- to gain a strong understanding of the witness of the Christian community as a vital element of catechesis;
- to emphasize the importance of participation in the Sunday Eucharist;
- to learn other methods for involvement in whole community faith formation.

The skill was to be involved as learners within the whole community so as to teach learners to do the same.

Session Twelve: Teaching within the Christian Family

The goal was to help you learn how to promote the celebration of the faith within the homes of learners.

Your objectives were

- to discover various strategies for involving families in the faith formation experience;
- to encourage means for the growth of the faith within the home, especially by helping families become communities of love;
- to involve family members in the sacramental preparation of learners.

The skill was to foster the spiritual growth of the learners' families and households.

Session Thirteen: Teaching through Apprenticeship

The goal was to help you learn how to find and prepare mentors to assist in the faith formation of learners.

Your objectives were

- to provide suitable mentors for learners;
- to clarify the role of mentors;
- to maintain contact with the mentors.

The skill was to prepare exemplary mentors to accompany learners.

Session Fourteen: Teaching with Faith Sharing

The goal was to help you learn to use faith sharing as a teaching method.

Your objectives were

- to grasp the dos and don'ts in leading faith sharing;
- to learn how to use examples of faith as a basis for faith sharing;
- to learn how to use questions to engage learners in faith sharing.

The skill was to engage learners in faith sharing.

Part Three: Review the Goal, Objectives, and Skill of Sessions Fifteen to Nineteen

Let these guide you in your review, as they are the main ideas, skills, and attitudes you took with you from these sessions. Read on your own or study with others.

Session Fifteen: Mentoring Others in Prayer

The goal was to help you learn how to guide learners in prayer, especially by praying with them.

Your objectives were:

- to be able to describe what prayer is, using Jesus as your model;
- to make the connection between prayer and the liturgy, the perfect prayer;
- to help learners develop their spirituality through prayer experiences.

The skill was to help learners develop their spiritual life, especially through your own example, the example of Jesus, and the liturgy.

Session Sixteen: Teaching with Stories

The goal was to help you learn how to use stories effectively in your religion sessions.

Your objectives were

- to value stories as a means of catechesis;
- to become an engaging storyteller, following the example of Jesus;
- to learn different strategies for using stories.

The skill was to become an effective storyteller.

Session Seventeen: Making Your Lessons Visual and Active

The goal was to help you learn when and how to use such aids effectively in your religion sessions.

Your objectives were

- to learn about various symbols and gestures that lead learners into the mystery of Christ;
- to become familiar with the different types of visual aids available for catechesis;
- to learn strategies for making the most of such aids.

The skill was to choose and use appropriate visual aids to stimulate the attention and imagination of learners.

Session Eighteen: Using Technology in Teaching

The goal was to help you learn when and how to make effective use of technology in your religion sessions.

Your objectives were

- to become familiar with the different means of communication available for catechesis;
- to teach about how the media affects culture;
- to learn strategies for making the most of this technology in and outside of the religion session.

The skill was to choose and use the most effective forms of technology to communicate the message of Christ to learners.

Session Nineteen: Teaching about Christian Initiation

The goal was for you to explore with learners the nature of Christian initiation.

Your objectives were

- to reflect on what initiation means;
- to teach learners about the lifelong journey of initiation and faith;
- to teach learners about the sacraments of initiation.

The skill was to help learners continue their faith journey, and to help you make that journey yourself.

Part Four: Exercises

The exercises in this section are not a test, although they will form part of your evaluation. They are a practical way of assisting you in absorbing and assimilating the material covered in this past year. In each section you will have two options. Choose one of the options and complete it as well as you can. Use your text, as well as any notes you have made.

Section I: *The Role of the Community, the Family, and Mentors in Catechesis*

Based on sessions eleven, twelve, and thirteen. Choose A or B.

Option A

1. What part does the witness of your faith community actually play in the catechesis of learners? Be specific. Are there ways in which you can build more on this witness? Explain.

2. List in detail three ways by which you involve (or will involve) learners' families in their faith formation. Why did you choose these particular means? How do/would you carry out these means? How effective are they?

3. Does your parish program include mentors? Why or why not? What is your vision of the role of the mentor? Choose a learner of a particular age level and be specific as to how the mentor might be involved in the learner's faith formation.

Option B

1. Name three parts of the Sunday Eucharist and explain how they offer a witness of faith to learners. Describe the importance of these parts of the celebration, and how you might incorporate them into your catechesis.

2. What are some aspects of a family's home life that are "catechesis"? Why are they so? How can you help families build on these?

3. Why is it important for you, the mentors, and the families to keep in close contact? Which means would you use to do this and why?

Section II: *The Journey of the Disciple*

Based on sessions fourteen, fifteen, and nineteen. Choose A or B.

Option A

1. How can you help form an atmosphere of trust and respect for faith sharing? What are some things you should keep in mind about the learners when you engage your group in faith sharing?

2. How have you presented Jesus as a model of prayer? Name some specific examples from the gospels and how you might apply them.

3. Briefly describe each of the experiences the journey of initiation includes. Choose one and offer specific examples of how you help learners experience it.

Option B

1. What are some forms of faith sharing you may use in catechesis? Explain what they involve and what their purpose is.

2. What are some types of prayer experiences you can use with learners? How and with which age group would you use them, and why?

3. Name some specific strategies you might employ to help learners grasp the connections between the three sacraments of initiation. Explain why you chose them.

Section III: Practical Teaching Aids

Based on sessions sixteen, seventeen, and eighteen. Choose A or B.

Option A

1. Choose a Scripture story and describe in detail how you would prepare to tell it.
2. Prepare an outline of part of a lesson in which you use a few of the symbols and gestures of the liturgy. Discuss your choice.
3. Select three of the means of communication and explain two ways you might use each of them during a lesson.

Option B

1. Discuss the effectiveness of using stories to teach. Give two examples for each age level (primary, intermediate, etc.) of how you might use stories during a session.
2. What is the purpose of using visual aids in catechesis? Prepare a brief outline of a lesson in which you use at least three different types of visual aids or activities. Explain your choices.
3. In what specific ways do the media affect our culture? Explain four strategies for teaching learners how to be more discerning viewers and listeners.

Part Four: Your Own Evaluation

After you complete the above exercises, note the areas you feel you need to return to for further study, explanation, or practice. After the session, discuss these areas with another catechist or teacher, or with your DRE or principal.

You can use these questions as a guideline.

- Did I need a lot of time to answer a particular question or questions? Why?
- Did I find others easy to answer? Why?
- Did I feel unsure about an answer or answers? Why?
- Was it hard for me to apply the points of the lesson to a teaching situation? Why?
- What area do I think I need to concentrate on most and why?
- What areas are my strongest and how can I build on that?